Interviews With Top Producing Insurance Agents

By
David Duford

Copyright © 2018 David Duford

All rights reserved.

ISBN:1724254146
ISBN-13: 978-1724254146

A Note From The Author

A Note From David Duford

First, thanks so much for purchasing this book!

My goal in compiling these interviews is to reveal to new and struggling insurance agents what top producers and insurance marketers do to achieve a lifetime of career success.

In fact, I believe the greatest takeaway from reading these interviews is the unusual opportunity to see how top producers end up being successful in their business. Surprisingly, you'll discover many similarities, including how most experienced difficulties early in the career, how many wanted to quit, and how through their hard work, pigheaded discipline, and determination, decided to push through their difficulties to sustain lasting success in the insurance business.

Advice On Utilizing The Knowledge Shared In These Interviews

Unlike many interview-style books or articles, you won't find me conducting a deeper analysis of certain thoughts and quotes from the interview subjects. I think the greatest way to learn from these top producers and insurance marketers is to read their story in their own words, and let their experience speak to you in its own unique way.

This book will provide you a multi-faceted example of what makes successful people successful, and will continue to serve as a point of reference throughout your career in insurance sales and marketing. but as you read through it throughout your career,

Once again, thanks for purchasing this book, and I hope it helps advance your success in the insurance business.

-David Duford

Table of Contents

Acknowledgements 1

How To Produce A Half BILLION Dollars In Final
Expense Production! 3

How To Produce $15 Million Annually In Employee
Benefits Insurance Sales 28

How To Sell $250,000+ A Year In The Final Expense Business 41

The ULTIMATE Guide To Generating High-Quality Referrals 61

How To Sell Annuities Without Purchasing Leads 86

How To Sell 1400 Medicare Supplements In 12 Months 98

How To Close 43% Of Your Final Expense Leads 116

Top Strategies to Sell Life Insurance Online 127

How To Sell Final Expense Over The Phone 141

How To Specialize In Selling Disability Insurance 159

How To Sell $280,000AP Of Final Expense Annually 172

Interview With Nick Williams, The Medicare Millionaire 192

Is A Career Selling Insurance A Racket? 209

About Dave Duford.. 221

The Most Incredible FREE Gift Ever 223

Acknowledgements

I want to specifically thank each of my interview subjects for their willingness to share their stories in this book.

Specifically, I want to thank each of the following:

Nick Williams at MedicareMillionaire.com - Thanks for sharing in great detail your entire face-to-face Medicare Supplement sales system.

Chris Grove - Thanks for sharing your ups and downs in the final expense business, and reinforcing the reality that success comes only to those completely committed.

Larry Schneider at DI-Resource-Center.com - Thanks for sharing your disability prospecting system with my audience, and how disability insurance is great market for new and experienced agents alike.

Cody Askins at SecureAgentMentor.com - Thanks for sharing your story and how agents can successfully sell final expense over the phone.

Jeff Root at SellTermLife.com - Thanks for all the personal help you've given myself and other agents in regards to developing a strong web presence.

John Dugger - Thanks for your posts at Insurance-Forums-com and convincing me to get into the insurance business.

Christopher Westfall at MedicareAgentTraining.com - Thanks for sharing your amazing story of success, and helping Medicare agents across the nation to achieve success.

Stephen Burgess - Thanks for convincing me that annuities can actually be sold to final expense prospects.

Alan Town at ASCFinalExpense.com - Thanks for helping me "think big" in the insurance business, and being an example of what fruits a lifetime of hard work can bring someone in the insurance business.

Claude Whitacre at ClaudeWhitacre.com - Thanks for being an early inspiration for "intelligent sales training," and providing tremendous value on prospecting, selling, and referral generation.

Nick Frumkin - Thanks for helping me understand the fundamental reality of process-oriented in selling and prospecting.

Jim Ward at WardServices.com - Thanks for sharing your business's fantastic success in the employee benefits market. I've enjoyed working with you these past few years.

How To Produce A Half BILLION Dollars In Final Expense Production!

Interview with Alan Town

About Alan Town, President of Agent Service Connection

Alan and his affiliates have written in excess of half a billion dollars in final expense sales since he began. That's $500,000,000! Also, Alan is the chief architect and designer of Colombian Life's successful final expense product. With Colombian Life alone, he has issue-paid in excess of $200,000,000 in premium. He is also the largest distributor for Oxford Life and Kemper's life products. He has been so for the last nine years with Oxford and the last five years with Kemper.

DD: Welcome, Mr. Town. Thank you so much for agreeing to the interview.

AT: Thanks for having me. I'm excited to be here.

DD: Could you tell us a little about how you got into the insurance business?

AT: Next week will mark my 30th year in the business. I got in back in 1988, by accident. I was a young kid, 23, trying to figure out what I was going to do for a living. I knew it would be some kind of sales. I was waiting tables at the time and had moved to Florida. I grew up in Rhode Island, and moved to Florida out of school. I thought that I'd go down there and mess around for a while in Clearwater. I wanted to play on the beach, wait tables, go to the gym, lift weights. Have a little fun for awhile before I decided to get serious about life. Move back to Rhode Island. Get what I figured would be a real job.

I found the insurance business by accident. It was serendipity. I follow John Maxwell quite a bit. He is a wonderful leadership guru. I study a lot of his books. He's a New York Times bestseller many times over. He talks about finding your "giftedness". Everybody has a gift. Everybody has something that they're very good at. Some of us get lucky and figure it out early in life. Some of us don't get lucky and don't ever figure it out. I figured it out when I was young.

I met a gentleman through a friend of mine that I'd made in Florida. This gentleman owned a company called Capital Marketing Group in Clearwater, Florida. They were an insurance brokerage company working in Medicare Supplements. They were a brokerage house. The owner of the company, he took a liking to me. He asked me, "What are you doing waiting tables? Why don't you get a real job?"

"Well," I said, "I'm trying to figure things out at this point."

"Heck, why don't you come on and see me on Friday," he said. "I'd like to interview you, get to know you better."

I did that. I went in with the one suit that I owned and my American Tourister briefcase. I had a banana and an apple in it. I just wanted to look like I was important, look like I could be a businessman. I figured out early in life that it's important to fake it until you make it. You have to look the part, you have to act "as if". So I acted "as if". I walked in there looking like a businessman, or at least I thought I did!

I had a great interview. The gentleman described the company to me. He told me what they were doing, what their objectives were. Capital Marketing Group was a marketing company, an FMO, hiring agents all over America. There were six marketers in there that time and he said he needed somebody else on the phone. Back then there was no such thing as the internet. We didn't have cell phones. Things were a little bit more difficult back in those days.

He took a liking to me. He handed me the sales brochures for his primary company. He said, "Take this home over the weekend, come back on Monday. I'm giving you a quiz. Take the initiative to learn the products. Dive in deep enough that I see that you are going to take this seriously. Do that, and that cubicle in the back there, where there's a phone and an empty chair, will become yours."

I spent the weekend on the beach, like I was doing back in those days. I had a sales brochure in my hand with rates, trying to figure out what insurance even meant. I knew nothing about the insurance industry, like all of us as we enter the business. It's a different language for us. It's amazing what you have to learn about health issues, chronic conditions, medications. It's a world that a lot of us don't think about. We have to hone in on it, become proficient at it if we're going to become real professionals within our business. It's pretty impressive to listen to some people talk of their knowledge. Diabetes, respiratory and heart and cancer, all these various things.

I came back on Monday. I convinced this gentleman that I had taken this seriously and I had a job. It paid me $18,000 a year salary. $350 a week plus benefits. At that point that was satisfactory so I went to work. Humble beginnings for most people, including me.

They gave me a list of agents and a canned script. Of course I had to make that script my own. I contacted agents on the phone, first determined if they were even in this particular market, then went into the spiel:

"Here's what we've got to offer, here's why it would be a benefit to have added to your portfolio. May I send you a packet, send you a sales kit? I'll follow up with you in a week. We'll review it and see if it looks like it might complement your existing portfolio." That's what I did. My task was to recruit agents and to get them into production.

I was never motivated by money when I was young. Money was not something that was in the cards for me. I was not ever supposed to become a financial success. I come from a blue collar family, upper blue collar, if you will. My dad never made more than $43,000 a year. My mom didn't work.

There were two other brothers in the house. We were a frugal family. I went to college but I quit. I was bored, I had no idea what I wanted to do, so I dropped out. I wasn't supposed to become anything super successful.

My story is similar to many great final expense agents right now. We're not Ivy Leaguers. You don't need to be an Ivy Leaguer to find great success and fulfillment in this particular space. That's why it's so special. I was able to become the very top recruiter marketer in this organization within a couple of years. What gave me incentive, motivated me, was money. This was an opportunity. I learned that I was going to be able to achieve great financial success.

DD: What advice do you have for new insurance agents starting out?

AT: I always encourage good agents, if they work within a successful agency, to become very friendly with their top people. Find out what it is that they're doing, try to shadow them, ask them questions. You're going to find that most of them want to help you. Most of them do want to. They don't want to be at the top all by themselves. They want others, they want the bar raised. They do want the accolades, but at the same time they want to be pushed. And the only way to be pushed is to have some folks that are nipping at your toes all the time.

I took that attitude. I never reached the level of success that he did in that agency, but back in '92 I was made an offer that I couldn't refuse. I was asked to go join another agency in Austin, Texas. So I packed my bags and moved to Texas. I went to work as the national marketing director for another very large insurance brokerage out there.

Medicare Supplements were hot back then. The Medicare Supplements business was instant gratification. It was a simple yes or no. We paid first year commissions that were upwards of 60% with about 10% renewal. But agents were taking advantage of that particular space in the very vulnerable senior citizen market that we were serving. They were replacing their business each year in order to get another first year commission. That is a very dangerous practice. In 1993, the National Association of Insurance Commissioners came in. They levelized commissions. Our commissions went from over 60% to within the range of 18% to about 22%, levelized for six years. That completely changed the landscape of the senior market. Agents were no longer able to get out there unless they had a strong renewal income. They had to generate enough in first year commissions to pay for their leads and still put enough money in their pockets to make it a worthwhile week.

We got involved with a company called Acordia Senior Benefits. They had a low cost Medicare Supplement, but they also had a product that they called a senior life product. The commissions on that product were 75%, with a 10% renewal through the 10th year. That's pretty darn good renewal and lot of first year commission for the deal. Our take on that was 85% for the FMO. We didn't have big agencies in the business back then. We were going after the personal producers. The folks that we were hiring were Medicare Supplement agents that were looking for other opportunities. They wanted to capitalize on big first year commissions using a simplified issue product. About six months into that product line and that relationship, we discovered that we were writing about a hundred cases a month with that senior life product, by accident. We didn't know anything about that particular business. It grabbed our attention and we got to thinking and got to talking.

There was a competing FMO out of Georgia that I had a relationship with. They were writing about 300 cases a month in that particular market. We got into communicating with him. We started to learn about this thing called final expense. Back then a lot of us called it burial insurance. We decided that we were going to take a look at this particular market. We found out that there was a company out there called Londen Insurance which owned Lincoln Heritage. That is a company that gets great accolades from me. I've got great respect for them. I've never done business with them and I never will, but I have great respect for them. They are the fathers of final expense. Jack Londen, who's no longer with us, was a great, forward thinking, final expense entrepreneur. He paved the way for all of us.

Another company that I had great respect for in those days was the Old American Insurance Company. Old American was doing various things with what they called control distribution. It was a career operation. They had managers with assigned territories and they were doing very nice things in final expense.

We started to study those two companies and decided that we could do this. We got to talking to different FMOs, different organizations. We found out about tens of millions of dollars of premium that was being written in this final expense market. And it was very under served at that time. There are a lot more seniors out there that are retiring with insufficient income than there are with sufficient income and assets to protect. So we decided that long-term care wasn't going to be the way to go. We wanted a simplified issue product. Final expense was, without question, simplified issue.

So we went back to our primary company at that time. We were writing very good Medicare Supplement business with them before the NAIC came in and levelized commissions. We had a great relationship with them. We were their number two FMO in the nation at that time. We asked them if they'd be interested in diversifying their portfolio. They were a health company at that time. We wanted to build a final expense program with them and they decided that it would be a good move for them. A. M. Best likes companies that are diversified. They like diversification within the portfolio. Health companies are typically more vulnerable than life companies and they frown upon them. They love life business. Diversifying would get a B+ rating with A. M. Best and they thought that this might be what it would take to get them to an A or an A-. So they agreed and let us build their product. That was the first final expense program that I was involved with creating.

We built a program with Pioneer Life Insurance Company out of Rockford, Illinois. They're no longer in final expense. They have been sold multiple times over and the president of the company is no longer alive. It seemed like it was almost overnight that we were writing 1000 policies a month weekly. We were able to build a brand new distribution.

After that was a fabulous company called Shenandoah Life Insurance Company. They had gained a great market share in final expense 20 years ago under the great direction of a good friend of mine, Jim Henson. He's still very active in business today. He was their chief marketing officer. Of course, eventually Chesapeake Life came into the business and they did fantastic things in the market. Many companies have come and gone since. We put together product back around '95 with a company called National States Insurance Company. I was the architect. I, with another firm that I was affiliated with back in those days, had the exclusive marketing rights to that program. We had a great run from them, built great distribution, and contracted great people.

There was a company out there called Guarantee Reserve at the time out of Calumet, Illinois. They had great market influence and they were doing great things. Through them, I've found a lot of the great people that I work with today. I'm not a big believer in a lot of advertising. Successful agents are successful for a reason and they're not looking for a new home. Successful agents don't need another company. They need you to get out of their way and keep throwing leads at them. That's what they want. That's what they need. They don't need new companies.

I've worked with agencies over the years that had the attitude of thinking that new deals automatically meant more production. New deals don't always represent more production. They represent more headaches, more challenges, more to learn! Most companies don't know what they're doing. When I analyze a product, product is only a part of it. Underwriting rates, commissions, they're important, but not the most important. Rate administration, that's what's important. Rate administration with a fairly priced product, good commissions, with very lean underwriting. This is the key.

I've seen so many come and go over the years. A very few have stood the test of time, like Lincoln Heritage and Old American. They've got high rates, but they have some magic in their sauce because they're very successful. No company writes anywhere near the kind of volume that Lincoln Heritage writes. This is not an endorsement for them, I don't represent them, but I have a lot of respect for them.

DD: *Describe your strategy around recruiting agents.*

AT: I built a myself a big name and great distribution for the most part through referral. Almost everything that I've built, I've done so by going after the largest and most successful producers with competing companies. I'm not interested in my organization bringing in neophytes, teaching them the business. What I do is I go after superstars and show them another opportunity, another mousetrap. I try to file them away, try to earn a little bit of their business. I try to get to the point where I'm earning 60% or 70% of their business with the appropriate product mix, lead generation and, of course, service. That's how I've built my entire company. There used to be card pack advertising way back in those days. Cellophane wrapped little envelopes containing about 50 different cards, sent to insurance agents all over America. In there would be a mix of offerings for all different kinds of product lines. They'd flip through there, find what they were interested in, and get on the phone. But I have found over the years that most of the people that are shopping for new product are people that have failed with their existing agencies. Don't get me wrong, there are reasons why people fail with existing agencies. A lot of it has to do with lack of support, lack of training. Lack of leads, lack of supervision, lack of inspiration, lack of motivation. It can go on and on. But if this happens three or four times you've got to look in the mirror and realize that there might be something wrong with you. You're not motivated or it isn't right for you.

I've built the bulk of what I do through referral. When I meet a top agent, I know that that top agent attends conferences every year. When they attend conferences, they make friends with people that live in other regions, other territories, other states. I'm always asking people for referrals.

"Who do you know, that isn't in your backyard, that wouldn't be in competition with you, that you respect?" I ask. "Do you think that they would benefit from this particular product?"

"Oh Heck," they'll say, "I've got three or four friends that I look forward to seeing every year. One of them lives in Houston, one of them, St Louis, Missouri, and another guy in Little Rock, Arkansas. We don't do business with each other, but we're buddies and our wives get together at these conferences. We look forward to seeing each other every year. We've been buddies for a few years."

"Why don't you give this guy a call?" I say. "Tell them I told you to call and tell him I said hello. Tell him I told you to look at this product!"

They have fun getting that kind of information out and they're not afraid to do it. As soon as you get on the phone with this guy say, "Hey, listen, a buddy of yours out of Houston told me to say hi to you, his name is Jimmy Jones."

"Oh my God, how's he doing," they'll say, "I haven't seen them in four months, since the day we were together at the last sales conference with Columbian Life!"

And we'll tell them, "He's doing great, man. And he's been doing very well with this program that we've introduced him to. We thought you might benefit from it. There's a couple of places where it may fill some voids. Let me tell you what those voids might be."

One of the keys to my success is the fact that I know my competition inside out. Agents must know their competition as well as they know the companies that they represent. You must know your competition inside out. You've got to become a student of final expense. The first thing that I ask an agent that I'm talking to is, "Who do you represent now? I want to tell you right up front how I could compliment your existing portfolio. I may not be able to, but there may be some areas where I could help fill some voids. Tell me who you represent."

Give them a reason to tell you immediately who they're representing, so that they take their guard down, else they're going to ask, "Who are you? I'm not going to tell you!"

Let them know, "I want to help you. I know the competition well. Tell me who you're representing and I'll tell you how I may or may not be able to help you get this taken care of in 45 seconds. I don't want to waste your time. I sell for Foresters, I sell for Transamerica, I sell for Liberty Bankers."

"Great!"

"Well, let me tell you what we can do with Columbian Life that you currently can't do with your existing companies."

Go in and talk about what those features may be. It's important to know your competition well. You need to be able to talk in an intelligent manner to somebody about what it is that you might be able to do for them with an additional carrier. Not only that, but it helps you to gain credibility fast with your client. The same thing goes for my agents. We want our agents to be able to walk into a house and say, "OK, you have a policy here with Americo. They're a great company. I know them well. They're in Dallas, Texas, they've been around for a long time. But you know what, our program here may be able to fill some additional voids. How long have you had your policy in place now? Two and a half years? you know what, that policy is as good as gold. Keep it. Guard it, protect it."

I'm all about trying to raise some additional coverage, if they have room in their budget for it. I'm not one to advocate for replacements when coverages are over two years old. It's dangerous. Once they get past that two year contestable period a policy is as good as gold. It's an interesting practice and sometimes there are good reasons to do it, but in general there are not. This is a judgment call that has to be made at the time of sale.

DD: *Can you describe the mentors in your life?*

AT: I had very good mentors in my life. It's important to recognize the leaders and the mentors in your life. I've learned from John Maxwell that if you have done well, it's important to give back to some of those people. Recognize the fact that you are where you are today because you had great mentors. They've cared about you, raised you, lifted you, poured knowledge into you. You are who you are today because of the people that believed in you. I have made it a point to go back and thank and recognize the many mentors that I've had in my life. The people that have believed in me. Ours is a lonely, difficult business. There are times when we get down on ourselves and we wonder, "Did I do the right thing? Is this for me? Can I do this?" It's a business that is won and lost between your ears. It's a mind game. You have to have great tenacity and great self belief in order to continue to sustain success in this business.

A great mentor of mine years back told me that you have not arrived in this business until you can live off your renewals. I love that. This is a game of renewals. This is what excites me in this businesses. The fact that when a sale is made, it's not only a paycheck on Friday, it's a paycheck eight, twelve years from now. When we write people that are 67 years old and they're in pretty good health, they can be with us for 15 or 20 years. It's important to think about every sale that you make. It's not simply a piece of business that's going to give you a paycheck when you're back in the next couple of days. It's also one that's an investment in your future. That's what this businesses is that we're building. Long term residual income. And that's the beauty of the business.

When I was 35, back in the year 2000, I was looking out there. I was wondering what I could have accomplished had I taken that leap of faith and stepped out. I was working as an employee for these other two agencies and doing very well for them, making a living for myself. And I decided that it was time for me to go out and do it. What others that I know, that I have worked for in the past, had the courage to do. Every entrepreneur and every agency out there needs to be commended for their entrepreneurship. It takes a lot of courage to step out of your comfort zone. I was in my comfort zone, I was making very good money, but I was riding the coattails of the agencies that I worked for. So I made the decision to go off on my own. I don't mind telling you that I was making $165,000 at the time. I had benefits, I had country club membership. I had a Mercedes lease. I was living well. I had a young boy at home, my wife was at home taking care of him. Life was good. But I knew that I had this burning desire to do it. One day, if I didn't do this, I would wake up at age 65 looking in the mirror wondering what I could have achieved had I had the courage to go off on my own. I wanted to never have that experience.

I hope that everybody that's reading this understands that. Take inspiration from this because our success is a choice. It's a choice based on good decisions versus bad decisions. That's all it is. Some people say to me, "I want what you have. I want to be like you when I get older."

And I tell those people, "It's pretty darn good. My life right now, it really is. I'm 53. I make a lot of money. I have great fulfillment. But you know what? I don't remember my thirties. I don't, because I worked so darn hard."

DD: My dad said the same exact thing. He had a chemical business in Atlanta. He doesn't remember when I was a kid because all he did was work. It was on his mind the entire time. I get it now. That's the inflection point that you're building towards. You're pouring your heart and soul into it.

AT: You bet. That's what happened for me also. I was raised up in the Northeast. Education is very important out there. There's a lot of great Ivy League schools up there. Their attitude is that if you haven't finished at least a four year degree, doors won't open for you. You're not going to make much of yourself. That was pounded into my mind. I never believed in it, but at the back of my mind, it was there. So it wasn't in the cards for me. But I saw people that were not educated making tremendous amounts of money in this business.

The beautiful thing about our particular business is that people can make great incomes doing things that are outstanding within and for their communities. It can be a win-win business that doesn't require a high outlay of money. It's a very simple business. We can, and do, run it out of our homes. It doesn't require a tremendous amount of money in order to make a great living. Many people make millions of dollars in this space. That kind of money can be made, but it's not realistic for most of the people out there reading this, and that's fine. That doesn't have to be the goal. The goal is happiness, fulfillment, a nice comfortable income. It's fine if your goal is to work three days a week in the field with paperwork on Thursday. Take Friday, Saturday and Sunday off, have three day weekends, that's fine.

That's not for me. You'll never call my office on a Friday afternoon at 4:00pm and not find me here. I don't have to be here, I can take Fridays off if I choose to. I choose not to because I was raised to believe that we are supposed to work full time, not part time. It's full time work. Monday through Friday, 9am to 5pm, 9am to 5:30pm, whatever it may be. I tell my agents to treat this like a full time job. They will find themselves blown away by what they're going to be making, with back end commissions and renewals, three and four and five years out. So treat it like a full time job. Get to a point where you have that great cushion coming in. It makes our lives so much easier and takes all that stress away as we move on through our careers.

I started my company back at the age of 35. I contacted my father back in Rhode Island and he said, "Listen, if this is what you want to do then you have my full support." It surprised me because I thought he'd say, "Are you crazy? You're making great income, why would you walk away from such a thing?"

DD: "Take the safe route!"

AT: Exactly. But no, he was all about it. It shocked me. He said, "Matter of fact, move back here, come back in to our home, move back in with Mom and Dad at 35 with your family. We've got room down in the basement." It was an old Victorian home with a dirt floor and asbestos wrapped pipes. "Put an office down there," he said.

And I did that. I sold everything and moved back to Rhode Island back in April 2000. I went to work 18 hour days in my dad's basement, dehumidifiers running like crazy, keeping the moisture away from computers and phone systems.

DD: It sounds like this was the burn the bridges moment in your career!

AT: You're not kidding! I was killing it. We were sharing a bedroom with our son. It was a small home. I had this 'we have no choice but to be successful' attitude. I had $150,000 to my name that I was able to save over the years working. At that point I'd already been doing well, but that's all I had. And I was scared. I spent $30,000 pretty quick getting my office set up. Computer equipment and phones, everything I needed, licensing, getting all that taken care of.

I found that I had a lot of loyal friends in the business. I was able to reconnect with so many people with whom I had relationships. This is a relationship business. People do business with people that they like, people whom they know have their back.

So many of the people that do what I do on the marketing side are not ethical. As an agency, you trust them with the most important thing that you have, which is your relationships. You have seven or eight people out there. You've poured time into them, trained them, and they now work with you. You support them and you bring them to an FMO. Then you find out, six months, a year, two years from now, that that FMO is now making other product offerings direct to them. Undercutting you. That is unacceptable. I don't play those games. I never play those games. I never will play those games. I don't need the business. I'm not going to harm people that have been good to me. I have always done things the right way. They were very quick to come back to me.

I started with Boston Mutual, back in 2000. I had a wonderful run with them. But like most companies, they're there today, gone tomorrow.

DD: Was this a final expense product that you're representing? I've heard of them, but I didn't know that they had an involvement in final expense.

AT: They had a wonderful final expense product that came into the market back in 2000. My timing was perfect. I was able to get in with them at the ground floor. I became their number one FMO almost overnight. We were writing over $6,000,000 a year with them in a very short time. I had a great run, made great friends up there, but it only lasted about four years.

Most companies getting into final expense are not serious about it. They have an ancillary interest in the market, they know of it, they want to taste it. They want to test it and that's what they do. Then they figure out that they don't want it. It's more difficult to make money in this particular space. They see that they're not meeting pricing expectations and they think that their mortality numbers might be coming in higher than that which they priced for. They get scared and pull out of the market. Why do they pull out? Because they don't need it. They are very successful in other areas. That's one of the very real concerns that we've always got when we get involved with a carrier.

When I started my company back in 2000. I contacted Todd Swenson to let him know that I left the organization that I was with. He was with Columbian Life at that point, he had left Security Life for that back around '98 or '99. Colombian Life had been involved with final expense at that time for 120 years. That's what they do. Their primary line of business always has been small face amount life insurance. That grabbed my attention. So I contacted Todd, and he said, "Alan, what I want to do is to fly you up to the Home Office in upstate New York. I want to introduce you to our president, our chief marketing officer, our marketing VPs. I want you to meet our head underwriter and I want you to take a work portfolio. I want you to consider coming to work with us."

I did that. I flew up to the Home Office. I was working with Boston Mutual and I was doing well with them, but I knew that this was a test market for them. At the back of my mind, I realized that this may not last. And I knew what I wanted. I was looking for that big hit. One of the primary companies that I could dive in deep with. So I got in with Colombian Life. I had a big interest in pushing hard with them. They understood (and have since day one) the small face amount life insurance business, blue collar market. This is what they've done since day one. So I went in there, met them, looked at their product, met some people, and decided that these were my kind of folks. They were not a giant company. They were small enough that you could get to know the people at every level. They were a mutual company that have been around for well over a hundred years. All they understood was small face amount life insurance.

The final expense program that they were selling back in those days had lots of flaws. They told me that they wanted me to revamp their products. They wanted my contacts. They didn't have the right distribution in place. Again, the market was relatively new back in those days. Columbian Life, as an example, was the first company in America to write an insulin dependent diabetic with full benefit. Everyone does it now, but they were the first. They had the stats back in those days where they knew what was eating on them. They knew what they could live with. These are stats that go back many years, that other companies didn't have. This enabled them to take a bold step forward. They gave me the opportunity to create and architect the next generation of final expense products with the company.

Todd and I were tasked to do that and that's exactly what we did. We completely redid their product. We came out with some very advanced underwriting. Very lenient, very forward thinking, very 'out of the box' underwriting. We would benefit diabetics on insulin. We would benefit people that were taking medications for a heart attack or stroke, or recent heart surgery, as long as those procedures or the actual event were over two years ago. Even if they were taking blood thinners, we could often give them a full benefit. So we built a product with which I was able to grab the attention of a lot of people very fast.

That was back in 2000. I've been with Columbian Life for over 17 years now. It has become my flagship company. Colombian Life and I have a super great relationship. I always tell the agents that they need to understand that the first winner must be the carrier.

The first marketing organization that I worked for had a different attitude. You write a company for as long as you can, and if it doesn't make money in a lot of the market, no big deal. There is another one in line to jump on now. That was a bad attitude, that if you get three to five years out of the deal you've done well. Move on to the next one. I learned how to recruit there, but I didn't learn how to care about my carrier.

The second company that I joined was out of Austin, Texas. They taught me how to care about my carrier, how to care about the company's bottom line. They understood the necessity for the company to be the first winner. The company must make money. If the company does not make money, you don't have a deal. You don't have a long-term view. He taught me how to care about the carrier.

To care about your carrier is to be careful about who you hire. You're only as good as the people that you recruit. He taught me that the best time to fire somebody is the first time that you think about it. You fire your failures fast. John Maxwell taught me that it's OK to say goodbye to people along this journey called life. If people are not on the same path that you're on, say goodbye to them. Get them out of your way. Get the naysayers out of your way. I'm a big believer in that.

I had great training and learned how to recruit through high levels of activity. Then I learned how to be very particular about who I recruited. I learned how to teach the importance of making sure that the first winner in the deal is the insurance company. We do that by not cheating. We do that by making sure that we are not overselling. We do that by making sure that we're writing quality business that we feel in our hearts is in the best interests of the consumer. That does meet underwriting expectations and that will tend to stay on the books for the long haul. It doesn't do anybody any good if a piece of business comes off the books in three months or even three years.

People need to understand what they buy. A final expense policy is a lifelong financial commitment. Say the client is 65. I hope that they are around when they're 85. That means that they're going to be paying this $58 premium 20 years from now, so let's make sure we put them into a premium that they can afford. What is their monthly income? You've got about $1200 to work with. You have no right to put them on a $180 premium. At all. It's obnoxious. It's self-serving for the agent and it's wrong. People with a $1,200 a month income shouldn't be spending more than $40 or $50 a month. We all know this to be true. You're all probably shaking your heads and agreeing with me because we're all guilty. We've all done this.

DD: It's not good for the agent either. They'll be out of the business within 12 months because of all the chargebacks they're going to get!

AT: You're not kidding. We manage the heck out of our business, but we do it in order to help the carrier and help educate agents. Agents that have high not taken rates or low placement rates tend to be overselling. We talk to them about that. We try to hone them in, to help agents to understand that they've got to write quality over quantity. If it doesn't stay, it doesn't pay. It's in everybody's best interest to write business that feels like it's going to stick long-term.

I went to work heavy dealing with Colombian Life. The timing was good because then Boston Mutual decided to get out of that market. The ride that I've had with Columbian Life has been amazing. It will continue to be amazing. Their management team is the same folks that were there 17 years ago when I joined the company. They're very consistent. They tend to advance people from within. We have a brand new president, who was with the company 17 years ago. He started out on the financial side and he's now the president of the company. The philosophy and the culture don't change. Everything remains the same.

You have to figure out what company you're most comfortable with. And I like having a number one first choice carrier. I like having a very large statement with a carrier. You have to have multiple companies in your bag. It's necessary in order to be able to serve all the needs that you're going to be running into. But it's great to have a first choice company that you hold in very high esteem, one that you're building a meaningful commitment with. One with whom you qualify for conferences year after year. A company where you can build a voice, that's served agents well.

It's very difficult to become an expert with four or five different companies. You can have a pretty good feel for those companies from 500 feet up. but you need to know them at a boots on the ground level. You need to know everything in order to be able to have that confidence to be able to service your people and to be able to make sales. In this space, the more you know about a company, the more confident you're going to be with that company. Therefore, the more you're going to be able to sell with them with conviction. Conviction is what sells. People can read that on you. I'm not smart enough to be able to be an expert with multiple companies. I do represent multiple companies, but I'm an expert on the product of one company. I'm one of the architects of the product as well. I helped build it. I helped build their websites. When we joined the company they didn't have a website. Most companies didn't have websites 15, 16, 17 years ago. It's been a fun evolutionary process.

DD: You have relationships with all sorts of successful final expense agents. You've recruited more than 10,000 agents. Based on your experience, what qualities do successful final expense agents and agencies possess? Is there any difference between an agent that's successful selling final expense and an agency?

AT: The most successful agents that I have are our agents that, number one, have a dynamite work ethic. It's important for agents to hone in on the care that they're most excited about. Get qualified for a conference. Qualify for at least one conference every year and build a name for yourself with that company. Make sure that company knows who you are and make sure that the marketing VPs know who you are. The percentage of agents in a field force that actually qualify for their sales conferences is incredibly small. I get excited about the top 10 agents, but I get more excited about every conference qualifier. They are within an unique fraternity of people. It's a very special group. People that qualify for conferences do not receive enough recognition for qualifying. You qualify for a conference, that means that you put the majority of your business with a specific company. That company has been enriched with your business and is thanking you by taking you and your guests to a beautiful resort somewhere. That's wonderful! That is a terrific way to say thank you. The agent's agency needs to realize how big a deal that is. It's a terrific honor to be among that particular group. So get qualified. Feel like a rockstar. Have that red carpet rolled out for you. I've been on every conference, I've worked with so many different companies over the years. Columbian Life puts together the best conferences I've ever been to in my life. The president of the company is there to greet your bus when it arrives at the resorts. He's not hiding upstairs in his suite, only to appear during an event. He's there to shake your hand when you get off that bus. He knows who you are because he's studied your picture before you arrived. It's a special appreciation for the things that you do in the field. I feel like that's critical.

DD: You're in the position of dealing direct with the most successful agents. That's more or less your approach to how you recruit. You also deal with very successful agencies. Do the qualities and characteristics needed to be successful align between agent and agency? Or is there a conflict between them?

AT: The characteristics that relate to what makes an agency or an agent successful are a little bit different. What makes an agent successful is, number one, having a terrific work ethic. You have to be smart. Given, you have to work hard. You have to have great discipline. You have to be driven. You have to be self motivated. Some agencies do a better job motivating their people than others. Some people just want to be left alone. They say, "Give me your leads on Monday morning and get out of my way. I'll tell you how I did on Friday." That's the way that some people want work.

The agents that are most successful are agents that are focused on one company. They are focused on trying to qualify for a conference. They know that when they walk into a house they're pulling out Columbian Life as an example. That's the company that they're most comfortable with. Sometimes there's a health issue that means that they can do better for the client with another company using a different product. Agents that are focused in on one or two products are in general the most successful. Agents that have eight or ten products in their bag with no real alliance with any carrier are the least successful.

As an agency, when you give your agents too many choices, you're confusing them. You're giving them temptation that is always taken when it comes to debit balances. I have three recent cases, both with carrier A. I now owe $1800 to them. Yet Carrier B, C and D are clean, no debt. Where do you think the business is going to go this week? I've got to make a paycheck. My mortgage is due next week. I'm $1400 shy of making that payment. I'm going to leave Company A alone. I owe them $1800! I'm going to go ahead and place my business with Company B. Then, as soon as I owe money to them, I'll move to Company C, then Company D. Before I know it, I've got a $6000, $7000 debit balance or more between three or four different companies.

Agencies that make that mistake run into large problems, fast. The agencies that hone in and encourage the majority of their business with one company do better. They don't give too many options to their agents.

You've got to have a guaranteed issue product in your bag. You have to have opportunities for COPD. Opportunities for when there are height or weight issues. You've got to have options for clients like that. Outside of that, most companies have very similar underwriting. Figure out who you are most comfortable with and make that company your primary focus. Agents that have clear direction know before they walk into a house which company they want to pull out. It's the company that they're trying to qualify for a conference with. Those are the agents that seem to do the best.

It's a big deal to get agents focused in on the company that you've chosen early on in the year as it relates to their conference. If you get behind for two, three, four months, early in the year, your focus is off. You want them to know what company it is that they are pushing for early in the year, in January. If you need $6,000 per month to get you there, then you had better try to write yourself at least $8,000 or $10,000 with that company that month. Give yourself that cushion because you're going to run into some snags at some point. You may have an issue with leads four months into the year. We may decide you're going to take some time off or you run into a slump. You want to always hit something higher than your objective. You've got to have your agents focused in. You want to create agencies that have great success. Agencies that are all focused in with a carrier.

The goal is to get as many of your people at the conferences as possible. We're all going to be there together as a team with our spouses and we're gonna have a blast. We're going to make it our company convention, not just the carrier's convention. We have this focus, exactly what I've been talking about, on Columbian Life. The nice thing about Columbian Life is that when you qualify for one conference with them, you try to qualify for all their conferences. They do such a good job. They make you feel so special. The agencies love it. I'm going to keep plugging Colombian Life because it seems to be the one that works the best. The bulk of the people that qualify for conferences are young guys and young girls. They have kids and they want to bring their kids to the conference. It's their one trip per year that they can look forward to. And Colombian Life's trips for the most part are by the beach. When you go to the beaches, the kids want to go. 12, 14, 15 year old kids. They want to be there. Columbian Life's a kid friendly conference. They encourage the kids to come. Most companies do not allow the kids to come. This is just intelligence. Most of the people that qualify for conferences are in their twenties and thirties. We have people in their forties and fifties as well, and even some in their sixties, but we have a tremendous amount of people in their twenties and thirties. They qualify for conferences and they all have young kids. It turns into one big family affair. It's a great time.

Get them focused in on a conference that will keep them focused all year. Get their spouses involved. Their spouses will be nudging them along all the time. "How did you do this week? Are we on track?" They want to go. That helps. Agencies that seem to focus in on one company for the most part seem to have the best agents. There's a similarity there. Agents that are committed to a specific company seem to do better than the ones that are all over the board and don't know where they're going or what they're going to pull out when they walk into a house. That kind of focus makes a big difference.

DD: When you watch the news, you can't help but see Amazon taking over the world, company by company, with their acquisitions or their technology. You see how 30%, 40% of the population are going to lose their jobs due to technological advances. There are concerns among salespeople regarding what's going to happen in the next 20 years.

Today in final expense, it's face to face sales. Will we even sell insurance face to face in the future, much less have a marketplace for it? Final expense is different from a lot of other lines of insurance. A lot of agents don't understand as they get into it that it's a different animal altogether. Where do you think we're going to be in the next 10 or 20 years? Is automation or technology going to have any significant impact on the current day to day approach that we use?

AT: Technology is certainly going to play a role. It's playing a role now. We are now, in some cases, selling electronically with some companies, using electronic apps. We have more and more call centers popping up that are doing well. There are more and more people using the internet now. In our lifetime, final expense will predominantly continue to be sold face to face the old fashioned way. We're dealing with a very simple minded group of folks. People that are not tech savvy. At the moment, the bulk of the people that we sell to, they don't use the internet. They don't even know what the internet is. They do not have iPads. They have flip phones, not smartphones. It's amazing if they know how to send a text. Those are the facts and that's our business. These people still want personalized service. I can't emphasize enough the word personalized. They still want somebody to come by and see them. To explain it to them. To point to exactly what it is that you're trying to explain to them. That kind of service can't be replaced over the phone. I feel very bullish about that. Final expense will still be sold predominantly face to face as it is today. With personalized service, holding these people's hands through the process.

I do, however, believe that there will be a greater demand for call center opportunity in the future. We do now have more and more baby boomers. Even though they're not making much money, they do understand and use the internet. They use a computer and they're not going to stop using the computer. This younger group of baby boomers will be great candidates for final expense, five or ten years from now when they'll be in their sixties. Even though they know how to use a computer, they still have very low incomes. We have more and more people that are retiring broke. Today more than ever. I don't believe that cycle is going to change.

DD: Direct mail is king in this business. Some agents have expressed concern that technology is going to overtake that. Do you see technology altering how we acquire leads?

AT: I do believe that we're going to generate more and more leads in the future through technology. Direct mail will continue to do what it's doing now. I have heard people complain and worry about direct mail for the last 10 years, but it's still king today. It's still the very best lead today in our particular space. Now, there are more people using the internet and more companies that are gathering strategic data that is being used for lead generation. There will be more lead companies that pop up in the future generating leads via the internet. But direct mail will still play a major role. I still believe that the bulk of the final expense business being sold in the future will still be eyeball to eyeball, through agent straight distribution.

DD: Alan, I know you're extremely busy and I want to express my gratitude for this sharing of your life experience in the final expense businesses. It's so important to a share this kind of training and experience with new agents, because there's such an unfortunate lack of it. If someone's interested in learning more about what you do, how can they reach out to you?

AT: They can find me on my website. They can contact me in my office. Agent Service Connection can be Googled and I can be found that way. My website is www.ascfinalexpense.com. My phone number is 941 907 9390, extension 3. That would get them direct to me.

I appreciate the opportunity to speak with you. In closing, what I'd just like to tell people is that I have nothing on anybody that's reading this, other than time. I've been in this business for an awful long time. I've watched it morph into something quite impressive. 15 years ago final expense was looked down on within the life insurance industry. It's now being respected in ways that I'm so proud of. I've seen that attitudes have changed. There's a lot of intrigue regarding what we're doing in the communities that we serve. We should all be very proud of that. The only thing that I can offer to people is that all I have on on you is time with the business. I'm no smarter. I am one of those guys that puts the blinders on. I don't get distracted. I know what it is I'm trying to accomplish and I run hard and I don't let anybody get in my way. I know my business inside out. If you'll take that same attitude, learn your business. Learn it inside and out, know your competition. Get the naysayers out of your life. Get them out of your way. Keep a clear mind and do the same things every day. My success is through repetition and yours will be the same way. Success comes through repetition. It comes to doing the same thing each and every day you get up. Go to work. Stay on that regimen. You will wake up in four or five years with this terrific renewals and back end commission coming in. You'll realize that if you don't work this month, you can still pay your bills. What a wonderful business to be in. I wish everybody great success.

How To Produce $15 Million Annually In Employee Benefits Insurance Sales

Interview with Jim Ward of Ward Services Inc.

About Jim Ward

Jim Ward is the founder and principal of Ward Services Inc, a family run national insurance agency. They help small and large employers with their insurance benefits. Jim started as a life insurance agent way back in the day in 1977. He got into the payroll deduction business in 1980. In 2017 alone, Jim's company worked with over 220 enrollers nationally.

DD: Jim, thank you so much for joining us today.

JW: You're welcome. I'm looking forward to the conversation.

DD: Me too. Let's go back to yesteryear and talk about how you got involved in the insurance business. Can you tell us a little bit about your background and getting there?

JW: After finishing college. I had a military commitment. I went to the US military academy at West Point and there, you have a five-year commitment. After three years, I had a medical problem and was discharged. I had a wife and three kids and was looking for something to do. A local agent here in

Columbia offered me something good. I was able to work with the South Carolina deferred compensation program with a state-sponsored plan. I was on commission but had no competition, so it was fabulous job. That's how I got started in the business.

A few years later, I got a call from someone with an insurance company asking me if I'd be interested in payroll deduction. Although I had a great job, I wanted to get into something where I was in control. Be my own boss. That's what I saw when I saw the opportunity to get into payroll deduction. I did that three years or so after I got started in the deferred compensation program. That's how I got started in the insurance business.

DD: What exactly attracted you to selling insurance to begin with? Did you come into it because you knew people in the business? Were you simply finding other work, like I was? How did you actually decide that insurance was the direction that you wanted to go in with your career?

JW: I was an athlete in college. I've always been very athletic and I took up handball when I was in the military. I got to know the guys that played locally. One of them was an insurance agent here in town. When I got discharged, he asked me if I'd be interested in working with them. I had a wife and three kids. I didn't want to go through the process of going around the country interviewing with large companies. So I went ahead and took the opportunity. It doesn't sound very sexy at all, I know, but that's how I got into the insurance business. One of my handball buddies asked me. I was always very math oriented and it seemed like a good opportunity to me. I'm thrilled, looking back on it, that I did it.

DD: As you described earlier, the main insurance line that you're in now is voluntary payroll deduction or VPD. Can you give us a basic explanation for those people reading, as to how the voluntary payroll deduction business works?

JW: You don't sell policies direct to people. You work through their employers. It's offered on payroll deduction by the employer to the employees. An important part to it is that, depending on the size of the company, it's typically offered on a guaranteed issue basis the first time each employee is offered the program. Employees and spouses that have medical issues or different problems are able to get a guaranteed issue, up to a certain limit of the amount of coverage or weekly premium.

A lot of it has to do with convenience and ease of being able to purchase the coverage. Paying for it is easier as well. You don't have to get letters in the mail, that kind of thing. You don't have to set up a bank draft or get quarterly or annual payments. It's all done for you. It's very easy. The ease and convenience of it have a lot to do with why it's been so successful.

DD: The payroll deduction market has been enormous in its growth because you buy your insurance through your employer. There's this implied third-party validation endorsement if you will. It's very convenient. Has the growth in the VPD market been substantial over the past 30 years since you started?

JW: Oh yes. It's been exponential. There were not that many companies, even in the insurance business, when I first started. There were not many people involved in it. It's now a pretty big portion of that business. Back in the day for me, having been an individual agent, if I had a week where two people bought life insurance from me, gee, that was a good week. We now have a couple of hundred people that work for us. In the fall when we're really busy, there's a six week period of time that we're writing 4,000 policies a week. 4,000 applications a week during the busy time. Some of these numbers I may be low or high in guessing, but that one's probably a low estimate of what we're doing.

DD: You've mentioned some of the benefits of VPD, like guaranteed issue. You help people who have preexisting conditions that would otherwise prevent them from getting fully underwritten coverage. What do you think some of the drawbacks are? There's no perfect insurance route. There are always going to be challenges. What are the kind of things that you tell new agents to expect? The challenges that they're going to have to deal with when selling voluntary payroll deductions?

JW: It's going to take time. With an individual sale, you're going to go in and see the person. You're gonna get a yes, a no, or a maybe, which you're going to follow up in a couple of days. With our kind of thing, you're working with corporate customers and ultimately the employees. They're the customer of the policy. We're providing services for the companies. We help them communicate the benefits that they offer to their employees. Then we help the employees make their choices. What medical plan they're going to take. What they're gonna do with different options within their benefits program. How much they're going to put into their retirement plan. All those kinds of things. This is an additional service that we provide. And then we actually help them get enrolled in all those products and programs. And we don't charge a fee to do that. We offer the voluntary insurance plans as our means of getting paid. We're helping the employees and then by helping the employees, the employees purchase voluntary life insurance with long-term care. That's the biggest product in our marketplace. Then short-term disability, accident coverage, critical illness. Those are the kinds of things that we're offering.

We have to do a real balancing act. We're there to help the employer to help the employees to understand their benefits and get it right. We can't be overselling our products and programs to the employees. We've got to be helping them buy what they want, what they need, and what they're going to keep. That's the magic of what we do. I'd say that as a company we do a very good job of not overselling. We make sure that our counselors are helping the employees purchase programs that they really want and need. Not overselling.

We've got four or five employees that work for us year-round in the public school system. They are on a salary but also get some commission because they're working in these school districts all the time helping new hires get enrolled. But that is the only exception to the rule that our counselors are all on salary. No kinds of commission paid. We don't want to have any emphasis that creates motivation for our people to be overselling to the customer.

DD: *Retail agents like me work with Mom and Pop across the kitchen table. It's a one call close in many circumstances. You find the need and then you sell the product and yourself. You either make the sale or you're down. I can*

imagine the situation you're in is totally different. There are multiple players. You have to sell to certain people in the organization, but you also have to keep the employees happy. They'll tell on you if the agents push too hard with what they sell. Could you describe, for the agent who has no experience in this particular market, how the sales process is different to a face to face direct sale? What's the time and place involved to get an account sold? What's the turnaround time to get paid? Who do you have to be concerned with when you deal with one of these large organizations?

JW: It can take years to close a deal. I can give you a first-hand case. Frank is a fellow that works with me in marketing and sales. We both played football where I went to college. That's how I know him. He's about 20 years younger than me, but he helps us with communication and a lot of our marketing stuff.

He's got a very good friend who's the head of HR for a very large retail organization in the southeast. They have about 10,000 employees. We have met with that friend a couple of times. It's been well over a year now. We've recently been back down there and it looks like they're going to go forward. At least with the test case in their distribution center. I have only spoken to them a couple of times, but Frank's been in communication with them for well over a year. This is the real key to success. You have to be patient. You can't be in a hurry to make sales. They don't happen fast. It takes time.

DD: That's true. The business to business set up for a service takes time. My father sold chemicals and it would take him years to sell the deal. There are contracts involved. It takes time to sell to people because it's a big decision. To move over from one place to another can be inconvenient when you're comfortable with someone.

Jim, how would you describe your ideal target client? Who it is that you want to do business with today? Does it differ from when you first started? Who are they? What problems are they experiencing? Are they big? Are they small?

JW: Of course, the more employees the employer has, the better the opportunity. That's what we're talking about. A 10,000 life group has got

10,000 potential people to buy programs. A 100 life group has 100 people. If I sell 10% of 10,000, I've got 1000. If I sell 70% of 100, I've only got 70. so size has something to do with it.

I have found that the best customers are the ones that have multiple locations that are spread out. The more of a challenge they have to communicate with their employees, the better our opportunity is. That's what we sell. We can help them with that challenge. We can send people out. One of our biggest customers is a large grocery chain all over Arizona with a couple of locations in New Mexico. They can't go out to every one of their locations to talk to all their employees face to face. So we do it for them. We do this in the spring because that's renewal time for all their benefits. It starts on July 1st. Every spring we go out to every single one of their locations and meet with as many employees that want to meet with us. We talk about the benefits and get questions answered. We help them to make decisions with regard to what they're going to do for the coming year. They're an ideal customer. They're fantastic to work with. They also think we're fantastic and do a great job for them. We've been going to their stores for 15 years. We send the same group of counselors. In fact, last year we sent 14 or 15 reps. Only one of them had not worked there for five years or more. We send them back to the same locations. So they're in a situation where Joe is going back to see Mr. Smith, the store manager of store number six. They know each other because he's been going there for 10 years. The employees know him. He has developed relationships and friends. Those kinds of cases are great because it's a great relationship.

There's a key to it. We know we have to sell things and have the employees purchase things, but we do it in a way that's positive for the employees. The store manager, in particular, loves us. All his employees are finding out about all of their benefits. If they have questions, they know that they can talk to Mary or Bill and they'll be able to answer those questions. And then we get paid for all of their life insurance with long-term care, short-term disability, critical illness, accident insurance. All the supplements to their basic benefit plan.

You have to be patient with this. I know some agencies or firms like us that take a 'do it now' approach. They may write a whole bunch of business the first year, but they don't have a very good reputation in the industry. I've seen where they have customers who turn over on them constantly. That's not a good way to be a running good business. Build it slowly but surely.

DD: You get those clients and you keep them, like you described with the grocery chain. 15 years. There's a reason why they stuck around. It's because you do a good job. They like the reps that come out and see them now. You don't take them for granted. It seems like these other agencies do. I imagine that if they start to disappoint the employers, that's where you come in. You take that business, like any other business competition. You've got to love your customers to death because they're the ones that put food on the table. They give you a nice lifestyle.

You've made a few comments on how much the business of VPD has changed. Thirty years ago it was completely different. Could you take us through how your business first started? How did it grow to where it is now? To where you're servicing these very large organizations?

JW: It's been a natural process. It wasn't a grand plan that I came up with. Even the fundamentals. I never expected my wife to be running all the finances. She runs the company. I don't run the company anymore. I'm still "in charge", but I'm not really. She's running the business. She oversees all the money. She makes sure that it's coming in from where it's supposed to come in and that we're paying all the people and organizations that we're supposed to be paying.

I've got two sons now that run the business with me. They were in high school and college when I first got started in the business. Now they're both very involved. Jeff, our oldest, runs the operations of the company. He oversees everything going on here in the corporate offices. We have about 20 employees here in the corporate office along with the 200 plus that are out seeing people. He oversees the offices here. He manages the enrollments as they're coming in and the interaction with the insurance companies.

It's been an internal growth of our company. We're all involved except for my daughter who lives up in New York City. The part that I feel good about is that I don't have to worry about loyalty. I've got a wife and two sons. The second son runs his own company, but he actually handles our smaller cases for us. He and his mother worked out how the money is split up between him and us. He does his own stuff, but he does as much for us with taking cases that are smaller and enrolling them.

DD: It's that old adage of hard work and elbow grease. No magic pills or potions. No secret weapons. Is that what you're saying?

JW: I just put my head down and went forward!

DD: And that's still how it is. I'm sure you've gone through ups and downs in your career. We all do, especially those who are very successful. There's a pattern of sticking to your dreams.

JW: Very much so in the first few years, and I'd say 10 to 15 years after that. It's been a natural process. In the last five years, we've seen exponential growth. An agent that we work with here in South Carolina works with us on the South Carolina school systems. They are our biggest customers. We started with one local school district back in 2001. Today we've got 33 or 34 school districts and 65,000 employees out of the 75,000 employees in the system here in the state. It's more than 30 different employers, but they're all in the same business. It's worked out for us. It doesn't matter if it's school district one or school district ten, they all have the same benefits. It's all done through the same systems and processes, with electronic enrollment and all that.

It's all the same for everybody. In the last few years, we have picked up some city, county, and state agencies as well. Grocery was our original targeted market and we're still in that, but the school districts since, and city, county and state governments here in South Carolina have been phenomenal.

A lot of it has to do with this partner that we have. He started with the one school district and we've built that with him. We did a good job for them. Then we got involved in some other things as well. We went to the other local school districts. There are two school districts here in Richland County. We started with Richland One and Richland Two and built over time. There was no plan. That's just how it's worked out.

DD: Was there a point in time in the earlier years of your career when something happened that elevated you? Was there a large customer that you acquired that took the company to the next level?

JW: Yes. When we first started, we got an opportunity. I was working deferred compensation here, but I decided to get into work sites. I got a list from an insurance company of the agents that work in medical and property in the state. I would drive around the state for three days a week and two days a week I would work at my deferred compensation job. I drove around and talked to these agents and I started getting some business from them. A person or two and I would do the enrollments. It was all small stuff at that time, but we got the opportunity to work with a pretty big agency down in Charleston. They had Piggly Wiggly Carolina. All the Piggly Wigglies in South Carolina were customers of theirs. That was a breaking point. We broke into the grocery industry with a nice big customer who was locally owned around the state. That went well. Grocery employees are ideal employees for us. We can help the employer to help the employees, then we help the employees with their voluntary insurance as well.

Food Lion is a big grocery chain. They're up in North Carolina. I called up there and got an appointment with the HR person there. He was one of the most delightful and terrific people I've ever met in my life. We developed a relationship.

We started going around to all the Food Lion stores in the southeast. That was our huge customer to begin with. I couldn't tell you how many employees they had, but they had a lot of stores and a lot of employees that wanted help. Back then we weren't helping with open enrollment, just voluntary insurance plans. We were simply a vendor selling a product. We weren't even providing any value added services. We got started a couple of years or so into it. We started doing benefit statements for the employers and employees.

That's something that I today count as a valuable service. It's my favorite way to try to start a new relationship with a prospective customer. We'll do a benefit statement for them and for their employees. It will show the employees that they're not making $40,000 a year. They're actually making $60,000 when you count how much their employer is paying extra for all of their benefits. Them making $40,000 is their employer spending $60,000. Maybe even more than that with all the different benefits that aren't coming out of their paycheck. Benefits that they're receiving through their employer.

DD: *All you hear about on the news is how in 20 years, automation and robotics are going to eliminate 70% of the jobs. Nobody's going to be working anymore, just laying around, collecting the check. When it comes down to insurance, and specifically your line of work, where do you think the business is going in the next 10 or 20 years? Regarding automation technology, do you think the process of selling insurance via the employer is going to be exactly the same or do you see any changes?*

JW: I'm very non-technical. Back when we first started we took paper applications and submitted the paper app. Everything took weeks. If I was a counselor today (I did the enrollments with these employers 25, 30 years ago), I couldn't do it. You have to be able to get on the computer. You go into the system. You don't take any applications or any information from employees with paper. It's all done on the computer with the counselor there signing them up for whatever they're doing. Their core benefits, or if we're helping with their 401K policies, that's all done online. Even the voluntary applications are now all done online.

It's a whole different world. But it seems to be working out well. We had a fellow here who's a great employee. He was in charge of the state's electronic enrollment system. He got to retirement age, he wanted to retire, then somebody told him about us. I don't know how he came about coming over here, but we talked to him and we hired him. He's been a fantastic asset to our company because he knows all the technology stuff. Nowadays you have to be "with it" from a technology standpoint or you're going to get nowhere in our business.

DD: With the enrollment business changing, are agents still going to be required to go out to see people in an area of employment? Do you see computerized technology eliminating them?

JW: A lot of people in our industry are scared of that. There's a company, I forget its name, that does everything online. It's all done online. You can sign up for your benefits online and you can buy the voluntary plans online. Everything's online. That's a direction that a lot of large companies are going in. That's how they do things. That's going to impact us. It's already impacted us. Employers are deciding that they'll do it all. Nobody has to talk to anybody, just go online. You can educate yourself, you can get yourself signed up. But there's an awful lot of people who don't want to have to try to go online and figure out everything. They don't want to have to sign up for all their different benefits, go through the technology, read everything and understand how their disability works and how their long-term disability works. It's a lot of stuff. That's the solution that we're providing. We help the employers to help their employees understand their benefits.

Is it a concern? Yes. Has it had any impact on us? I'm sure it has. We might do less business, but then think about it, if we didn't have the technology, we wouldn't have this streamlined aspect to what we're doing. We wouldn't be able to do it as quickly and easily as we're doing. So even if we had more opportunity, we'd have less business because it would take so much longer. That's part of the deal. You definitely have to be into technology. Everything is being done on computers.

DD: General insurance is not like selling a car. No offense to our car salesman brethren, but most people look at a car salesman as an impediment to buying. They can see and conceive of ways to do it without them. Looking at some studies done, that doesn't seem to be the case with selling or buying insurance. There's some that don't want to deal with an insurance agent, sure, and they will have a reason why. But a lot of people do want the assistance of an agent. You need to figure out a way to differentiate yourself. You, Jim, emphasize the servicing aspect. You can help these companies identify ways to control that. That's an immediate

advantage to the company, but at the same time, you can help employees source good quality coverage. By being there face to face you can answer these questions. It's a lot better than being given a five, six, seven-page report on how it works and told to pick what you want. It's good to deal with somebody who can make the complicated simple. For those agents that do that, there's always going to be work.

JW: I agree. We have a call center here that we can staff with up to 12 people in the booths. We have two full-time customer service ladies. Employees and employers can call them with questions, if they want to purchase something, or if they want to make a change in their benefits. It's not all being done face to face. We are doing a good bit of work here. We're staying pretty busy with those two full-time people. We've got customers all over the country. We're doing cases where we enroll people in let's say California. We'll have a couple of people that are out talking to the employees. There's some that can't get to wherever our people are meeting with them. They'll call the call center and we'll take them through whatever they need to get done that way.

We do several thousand employees a year of new hires here in the school systems in South Carolina. We'll send people out to do those with the schools, but then we've got new hires that we're doing for a customer in Montana that we have. It's not frequent enough that we can send someone out there. When that Montana employer has employees for open enrollment they give them the information and then tell them to call this 800 number. Then we will help them to go through the process. We answer their questions to enroll in their core benefits and get on their benefit program.

DD: *Jim, some of these people reading this right now are going to be new to insurance. They want to be successful and reap the fruits of their productive labor. As you and I both know, the turnover rate in this business is enormous. 90% or more are not selling insurance after the first year. What advice would you give a newer agent on what they need to do to see the kind of success you've seen in the field whilst growing your business?*

JW: It's pretty simple. Just go at it as if it's going to be your career. Be focused. Try to understand, study and work at it and look at it as a competition. My dad was a college football coach and it was all about winning and losing. He had good years, he got promoted or went somewhere else. Bad years, he had a couple of those and he got fired. That's how I see our business. You have to learn, study, get up, have a plan, be organized, diligent, disciplined. Go out and see people and try to do the best you can. Help those people. That's one of the most important things. I know we all when we first started thought, "Well I have to be able to pay the bills," but you have to look at it that you want to provide the best service you can to the people that you're calling on. You have to give them real value because in the long run, that's how you build your business. We haven't built our business here because we're out shamming people and making a lot of sales. We've built it because we're helping people and they appreciate the help. They like it and they like the products and programs that we're selling. We've got competitive pricing with companies that do a good job servicing their businesses as well.

DD: Thank you so much for joining us today, Jim.

JW: Thanks for having me, David.

After 40 years in business, Jim Ward, his wife, and sons operate Ward Services, with over 200 full- and part-time employees and do business in approximately half the United States. You can find out more about Ward Services at www.WardServices.com.

How To Sell $250,000+ A Year In The Final Expense Business

Interview with Nick Frumkin of Final Expense Contracting

About Nick Frumkin

Today I have the pleasure of interviewing Mr. Nick Frumkin. Let me tell you a bit about him. He's been selling final expense exclusively for the past three years or so. As of last year in 2017, Nick sold a total of $287,000 in the final expense business alone. I'm speaking to Nick today because he's an excellent top 5%, if not top 2%, agent. He has a lot of good experience that's practical. In today's interview, we will be mostly talking about tactics. What Nick does to get into the home, what he does to sell the final expense product, dealing with objections and so on. If you're looking for information that's geared around training and doing implementation to improve your effort in front of your prospects, here is where it's at.

DD: Nick, welcome and thank you so much for joining. Let's start from the top. Can you tell us a little bit about your background and how you got involved in selling insurance?

NF: To cut a long story short, I was not in the insurance field until about five years ago. I was working as a teacher. My wife and I, for a variety of reasons, decided we needed to make some changes in our lives. We moved to a different state. There, I decided that I was not actually as fond of teaching as I thought I would be when I got into it. I wanted to try something a little different, but I didn't know what sort of skills I had.

My father is a financial planner. He deals mostly with annuities; 403Bs and things like that, so I've had a little bit of exposure to that kind of life. I thought I would see what's going on. I put out some feelers, got hired by Combined Insurance. At the time it felt like a really big deal. I realize now that they'll hire anybody, but they were a good training ground. I learned to sell to the lower to middle-income market there. I have ended up transitioning into final expense through a series of misadventures.

DD: I always find it interesting talking to final expense agents because it's not the first thing a lot of agents get into. They hear about it, they stumble across it. It isn't the first line of business on many people's minds to get involved in. How did you end up in final expense? How did you find out about it?

NF: I was doing pretty well at Combined Insurance. I met a bunch of people that worked there and had gone on to do other things. After spending a couple of years there, I started getting some phone calls from people trying to recruit me to do other stuff.

One day I got a phone call from a friend of mine saying, "Hey, I've started doing this new thing." He was always doing a new thing, but this time it actually sounded like it was pretty interesting. He said, "I'm selling final expense life insurance. We're selling to the exact same clientele that you're already working with at Combined Insurance. Instead of selling to these people when they're 30 to 50, we're selling to them when they're 50 to 70. The big deal is, instead of making 35% on a life insurance sale, we're making 80%."

"Wow, 80%! My gosh! That's amazing!" I said. "I'll at least come out and check out what's going on with that!" So he took me on a ride-along. It did seem exactly like what I've been doing for Combined Insurance, except that he had leads which we weren't allowed to use with them. Fortunately, I had decided that I didn't particularly like or trust his boss after talking to him. I thought that I should take the idea and see if there was somebody else out there that was doing it. I did some Googling and I found the insurance forums. When I found them, I realized that 80% was not the best contract that I could get. I talked to a whole bunch of different IMOs. I ended up talking to Scott Burke at Final Expense Contracting. I had a nice long conversation with him where he convinced me that they would treat me fairly and honestly. They would be a place where I could learn how to do this. That's how I ended up here.

DD: *Now that we know how you got into final expense, let's discuss what kind of schedule you have. Day to day, week to week. When do you start setting your appointments? When you run your appointments? How much are you working to set up appointments and see people in the field in any given week?*

NF: It should start with my leads. I am on a lead program where I have a set price lead and I get 25 of those a week on Friday. I put them into my CRM system. I set up appointments almost exclusively. I'll door knock if I need to, but not very much anymore. I start calling people at 9am on Saturday with a goal of setting a minimum of 8, maximum 11 appointments for Monday. If I try to set 12, things actually tend to not go very well at all in my days. Usually, I set 9 or 10. It takes me until 10:30am, about an hour and a half. I'm calling the fresh leads. My goal on Mondays is to give 10 presentations. It's a high bar. It's not always possible, it's not always even close to possible, but that's the marker that I've set for myself. I know that by the time I leave the field on Monday, I have done everything necessary to put myself in a position where for the rest of my week I don't need to work as hard. I can let the rest of the week take care of itself.

DD: *There's a couple of things there that are interesting to dive into. You call on Saturday, you set appointments. You don't door knock. Do you feel that appointment setting is superior to door knocking? Why do you do that?*

Why don't you take the leads and go out on Monday morning at 9 am and knock on doors to give presentations?

NF: For me, it is definitely superior to door knocking. I have a higher comfort level when I'm in somebody's house if I know that I've spoken to them before. They've said that it's OK to come on over. I have a lot of experience going into people's houses completely cold. That's what we did at Combined Insurance. That's their whole model. You don't get leads, you don't talk to people in advance, they drop you off in the middle of a town and you go sell stuff. It's a hard way to work. It's tiring. I do feel that I want to push to try and get as many of those presentations accomplished on Monday as I can. I'm lazy and I don't want to work very hard the rest of the week. I would like to work really hard one day and work less hard the rest of the week. For me setting appointments is about efficiency more than anything else. And my personal comfort level.

DD: I'm on board with everything you're saying. That's how I prefer to run final expense leads. But people who set appointments face a level of difficulty in getting some of these leads to pick the phone up. Sometimes only one out of four leads will. You can call them a million times and they'll never pick the phone up. The only way to see them is with door knocking. What are your experiences with the difficulty in getting people to pick up? What is the percentage that you actually set as appointments?

NF: Sometimes it is hard to get people to pick up. I have a theory that different cities and towns have different personalities. The culture of different places where you work can be tracked pretty clearly. There are places, if you drop leads there, nobody's ever going to answer the phone no matter what you do. And there are places, if you drop leads there, everybody's going to answer the phone. But nobody's going to show up to their appointments. There are places that are in between. I have, over the last couple of years, tried to eliminate places where people never answer the phone. That's step one for me. As far as the number of people that I actually contact goes, off of my 25 leads, I'll usually run 15 to 18 appointments every week. I'm getting appointments set with a good number of people. I've never thought about the numbers that

I'm not reaching. I do door knock if I have time. If I'm out in the field, stood up by somebody or I have a couple of short closes or no sales back to back, I'll go out and fill that time. I'm not sitting around in my car reading a book.

I don't have as much difficulty with the people refusing to answer the phone as other people seem to. I don't know if it's because I'm more persistent about it. I continue to call. I have no problem calling people on the same phone number 8, 9, 10 times in a day. A lot of times I set appointments after I'm done setting appointments. People call back and they're saying, "You called me five times today. What's going on?" That happens too.

A lot of new agents, when they get into this, they get discouraged by small samples of calls. They have something bad happen to them four or five times. They'll have two or three days where they have a rough call day. It happens to happen at the beginning of their career. It happens to everybody, but they decide, "This is not for me, that's never worked. I don't know how anybody could do this!"

There's a long track record of sitting down, making the calls, putting in the time and setting appointments. It does work. Not only in my own personal experience but also that of the people that mentor me, that I've worked with and talked with. It's significantly more efficient. I spend a rough total of two hours a week setting appointments. Tops. On a bad week.

DD: *Do you think that calling Saturday mornings gives you a slight edge on how many people you're reaching?*

NF: For me Saturday morning is the best day to call. I call 9am Saturday every week. There is very little that will keep me from getting on the phone at that time. I know guys that call Monday and Wednesday and set appointments for Tuesday and Thursday if they have fresh leads. I have no problem with that. I know people that call Sunday night. There are some people that say, "Forget it. Saturday mornings are not happening for me," but they sit down 4 or 5pm on a Sunday and call and they have no problems. For me, Saturdays are the best time. You get these people on the phone and you set appointments.

DD: A lot of the final expense community will say that they call to set the appointment. If they sell anything, it's selling the appointment. It's not selling the product. Some people do some qualification on the phone. What's your approach when you set an appointment?

NF: I don't want to qualify at all. The less I know, the happier I am. I don't know what the people who do a lot of qualifying on the phone talk about in their appointments. I would love to sit down and talk to one of them someday and find out how their appointments go. I don't understand what they could be talking about. That's all my appointment is; qualifying. I sit down and say very simply "Hey, I'm the guy you sent this card in to. I'm going to be in your neighborhood Monday at 10am. Are you going to be home?" There's a little bit more to it than that, but not a whole heck of a lot. I'll verify their address, but that's it. I don't want to know anymore.

DD: That's the easiest way to set appointments and it works well. We're talking about the direct mail program, which we'll get to. A lot of agents think they should do some other kinds of leads. What kind of objections do you hear when you're calling on the phone to set appointments? What do you think the most common one is and how to handle it?

NF: The most common one doesn't get talked about a lot. It's when the client claims, "I didn't send that, that wasn't me."

DD: "That's my signature, but I didn't send it!"

NF: Yes, "It wasn't me. I didn't do that."

I slow down and read the card to them. I find that a lot of people knee-jerk, thinking that you are calling about something completely different. They don't even listen to you for the first couple of sentences. To me, that's an indication that I'm speaking too fast, which is a tendency that I have, especially on the phone. They're not hearing me. I can keep them from saying that they didn't send that and putting the phone down. I stop and say, "Well, this is, I think, something different. I do have this card in front of me. This is what the card says," and I read the card back. If all else fails say, "Well, I'm going to be in your neighborhood anyway. I'm still the guy that's supposed to get this to you, are you going to be home on this day? I'll show you the card when I come by. I promise you that I have it. You did this, this was something you wanted."

The other objection that I get a lot is, "Oh, I've already taken care of that," or "I already have something. I already did that. You're too late."

This is actually a good one. Those are people that you want to see. It's as simple as saying, "That's great! That's not a problem. You know, most of the people that send this card in already have something taken care of. That's not why I'm calling. I'm calling because you requested this information and I'm the person who is supposed to deliver it to you. I'm going to be by on Monday. I just need to make sure you're going to be home. Will you be home at 10am when I come by?"

90% of the time that's enough. It's not a big deal. Sometimes you can go into other stuff, but most of the time you don't need to do anything more than say that you're coming by anyway.

DD: When you hear that they have insurance, you're not asking who they have it with, or the price?

NF: No, because that'll scare them off. If somebody tells me they have insurance, those are people that I want to talk to. They have proven that they are interested in insurance. They've proven that they can pay for and keep up with their insurance policy. That's definitely someone I want to talk to.

DD: Pro tip for you new guys out there. Remember the old saying: "The best person to sell a policy to is the one that's already paying the premium." Many times you can improve their lot with the insurance that they have. So don't get discouraged, do exactly what Nick says and see them anyway. You'll be surprised how much more business you'll do.

Let's talk about leads. You mentioned that you do a fixed price lead program. Why do you work them rather than other kinds of lead sources? What would your comments be to agents that prefer to use something else? If they want to use a non-direct mail lead card as it relates to their longer-term career aspirations?

NF: I've used a lot of different types of leads over time. I've used a lot of different telemarketers. I've experimented with using Facebook leads. I've done a bunch of stuff.

Direct mail is the only lead source that I've worked that has been consistent in the number of leads and the quality of prospect that it delivers. Even if you're paying $33, $35 a lead, they're cheap in comparison to the return that you're making on those leads. Let's say you're only on 100% contract. You probably do better than that, but a lot of people don't. If you're making $4,000 a week, you're spending $600 on leads. With that return, it's silly to not get the best quality lead that you can get. At a certain point, you have to bet on yourself and believe that you can do that.

There are other lead sources that will be good in the short term. I like telemarketing leads as a fill-in lead. If something happens, I'm paying price per lead, so it's not a big deal if I don't get all my leads in. I'm not paying for them. Every now and then it happens that I get five leads. It's not my favorite thing, but it happens. Telemarketing leads are good to fill in. They are inexpensive, they come fast. But anybody that's worked a lot of telemarketing leads can tell you two things. One, they burn out fast. You can't call the same area very often. You start having to expand your area and pretty soon you're working your entire state. I live in Pennsylvania. That's a large area to work.

Two, you get a lot of people who aren't interested. They say yes to get the telemarketer off the phone. You get a lot of people who don't know what they're talking about. They are suffering from dementia and other types of psychological disorders. And you get a lot of people who are deathly ill. You don't get that with direct mail. You don't have to worry so much about area burnout. I've been working the same area now for more than three years. The returns are the same today as they were when I started. I get some repeats, but not near as many repeats as some of the people that I hear complaining.

DD: You guys that are new, you'll find that as you spend more time in the final expense business, you'll develop an interest in trying to find something else to substitute the direct mail lead. To see if there's something better. I can relate to what Nick is saying. I've been doing this since 2011. The way I

generate leads is exactly the same today as it was when I started in 2011 when I was told to buy direct mail. I didn't have the forethought to think otherwise at that point. I was doing what I was told. It's funny how you go back to basics after experimenting with other things. I agree that there's definitely a place to have those leads as fill-ins. Nick and the people he works with, these guys have been doing final expense for ages. There's no sex appeal in this business. We're doing the same old thing. It's all direct mail.

NF: You mentioned that you were doing what you were told. I find that the guys that are most successful when they're starting off are the ones that don't think that they know any better. They do what they're told to do. There's a lot of guys doing the telling that have been doing this for a long time. They have this business figured out. They have been very successful. Everybody says, "Don't try and reinvent the wheel." Those people aren't trying. It's a good business. You don't need to reinvent the wheel. This business already works the way that it is.

DD: *It's so easy, It's complicated. If you have a creative element to you, you've got to find another outlet for it. Otherwise you'll start going in and tweaking this business. And what's so weird about this business is that it's already been figured out. All you hear about in the news today is how technology is interrupting everything. Amazon is destroying the basic retail model. Insurance is dramatically changing. But we're doing the same thing that these guys were doing in the seventies and eighties. It's practically the same kind of lead card. It sounds crazy, but that's how it is. I don't think it's going to change that much either.*

NF: I don't either. It doesn't look like it's going to change. I've only been working with final expense for three years. I've been doing other stuff for a couple years longer than that, in more or less the same market, with younger people. The biggest change that I've seen is the rise of cell phones and texting. My clients would rather text me now than call me. That's it. I've talked to other guys a lot. I try hard to talk to as many people as I can. I'm a big believer in surrounding myself with smart people who are better at things than I am. It seems to be the same for everybody else. There's not that much that's changing. I've tried using some of these Facebook leads that have become popular and they're fine. They're more expensive than a telemarketing lead and they seem to be about the same quality. They don't, for me, bring in a different type of prospect. They're not as good as direct mail.

DD: A raging debate that you'll get into with agents over direct mail is whether or not the lead should say life insurance on it. What are your thoughts on that? What do you use? Does it say life insurance, does it not? Where do you stand on that?

NF: My feelings about this are somewhat complicated. I use a lead that says life insurance. In the area where I'm working and with the way the lead house that I work with sends out leads, I get too many leads if I do not put life insurance on them. By the time I get to them, I end up starting to work leads that were returned in September when it's now January. That causes problems, so I needed a way to cut back on the lead flow, especially as I'm dropping price per thousand. There are some good lead houses that do drop the price per thousand.

For a new guy, I would recommend a lead that does not say life insurance on it. You want to get your returns as high as possible. If you're getting a fixed price lead and you don't care that you're working three or four-month-old leads, don't say life insurance. You'll get way more leads. People tell me that I will get fewer people who already have life insurance if my lead says life insurance. I ran the lead connection E64 lead for two years. I've been running the lead that I've got for about one and a half years. I started with it not saying life insurance. Now, I've been having life insurance on my lead for a full year. I have not noticed any difference in whether or not people have life insurance already. My replacement percentage hasn't changed at all. I can't tell the difference. The number of people who think it's not about life insurance hasn't changed either. Everybody still says, "I didn't know this was life insurance!" It doesn't matter that it says life insurance on it. But you will get fewer leads back. For me, that's a good thing.

DD: It sounds like part of the reason that you do say life insurance on your leads is to make sure your leads are still fresh at the time you get to them.

NF: Yes. There are many people who will tell you that it does not matter at all. I personally have noticed that the lead gets a little bit harder to work when it starts to get to be about three or four months old. Even if you've never contacted them. It doesn't matter so much that you can't sell to them, but it matters a little bit. Also, the lead house that I'm using starts to get mad at me if I end up with a backlog of 1000 leads that I haven't paid for yet. They shut off dropping fresh leads for me. They say, "You've got too many that we haven't." It's a problem, but the best problem to have!

DD: Now let's jump into your actual sales presentation. I'm sure my audience is interested to hear what you do. Let's talk about rapport building. Some guys do a lot, some do very little. What do you do? You also sell a little bit of other product besides final expense as it presents itself. Is your presentation laser-focused on final expense? Are you doing more of a generic factfinder to collect these other business cross-sale opportunities?

NF: As far as warm-ups go, I am a big believer in the idea that most of the people we're sitting with don't have much of an attention span. You've only got a couple of minutes to grab them. You shouldn't go in there and be rude, you shouldn't go in there and not say things like, "Hello, how are you doing?" However, a greeting is the extent of my warm up unless there is something that I see in their house that is cool. I saw a guy the other day who had this five-foot long model airplane that he had built himself. That's awesome. We talked about that for a couple of minutes. But the reality is that most people, in my opinion, do not care who I am or what I'm there about, other than to have the meeting. My whole purpose when I'm in their house is to be as professional and efficient as possible. I try to give 10 presentations a day. If I'm in each presentation for more than an hour, I am in trouble.

A lot of times people appreciate me being direct and very straightforward, not being salesy. I'm coming in and saying, "Hey, how are you doing? I'm Nick. We talked on the phone the other day. I'm here to talk about the final expense programs. Do you mind if we sit at your table over there?" Go sit down and go into it, "I'm here. You sent this card back."

DD: *Are you jumping into a strict final expense presentation, or are you collecting facts along the way for potential other cross-sell opportunities?*

NF: I do some cross-selling in a couple of different ways. It's pretty subtle how I collect that information. My presentation is a final expense presentation. When I introduce myself, say who I am and what I do, I say, "In addition to final expense my company does help seniors with other senior benefits. We do things like Medicare, help people with retirement plans and so on. That's not what I'm here to talk to you about today, but if in the future you'd like to talk to me about something like that, we can do that." Then I go into my regular final expense presentation. When I'm asking people about their health, I ask people what they use for their health insurance. I find that's a natural place to put that in there. It gives me an idea about whether or not there's even a reason to be talking to them about anything else.

I look a little bit for Medicare stuff that way. Anything else that I sell above and beyond that is going to be based on the fact find that I do during the final expense presentation. They've got a universal life policy that has $20,000 in cash value in it. I'll talk to them about some things that they can do with that cash value. If you do not know how to do it, don't do anything other than offer for them to get the cash value back. I have a background in doing stuff like that, so I can recommend some good single premium products. I can recommend an annuity.

My presentation is very much built around the idea that this is a conversation that I'm having. There are very strict points that I'm hitting. There are very specific marks. There is room in my presentation for them to ask me questions, me to ask them questions, and to establish a little bit of rapport as we go along that way. I use it to find out if there is genuinely anything that they need. Before I leave everybody's house, if for some reason the Medicare stuff hasn't come up, I will say, "We do help people with Medicare. If you ever want to talk to somebody about that, when you see the commercials come on TV reminding you about Medicare and you think that you should do that, pull my card out, give me a call. I work with all those same companies also, I'm more than happy to sit down and talk to you about it."

I get calls from that not infrequently. When I was with Combined Insurance, I spent most of my time in their Medicare. I didn't start off there, but that's where I ended up. I came into final expense very familiar with Medicare because I worked for my father as a teenager and then a whole bunch of other reasons. I understand how things like single premium whole life insurance, annuities, that sort of stuff, works. I've got a better grasp on that than your average Joe. Those are things that I'm very comfortable talking about. I strongly recommend for new agents, if you do not have that background and you do not have that comfort level, that the best thing to do is to focus on one thing. Get good at selling final expense. Start selling $200,000 in final expense a year and then learn how to do something else if you want to. For me it's not any extra work. It's not anything that I have had to learn. It's something that I've been doing for longer than I've been doing this. All of that said, 85% of my business is still final expense.

I like doing Medicare stuff. I get a lot of referrals for Medicare stuff. But Medicare is not my line. Medicare is something that I go to if I happen to stumble across it. It's the same thing with single premium and all the rest.

DD: As soon as a new agent gets out there, many times they find there's all sorts of other sales opportunities. On some level they feel like they're losing out on business. But I find that diffusion is the enemy of productivity. If you're a new agent, you will find that it's enough to know five or ten different insurance companies as they relate to final expense and underwriting. It's difficult to understand the final expense market. You don't need to throw a whole new problem on your back. At least, not until you've actually proven that you can write substantial business and do well. Like you said, you may not even care if you're not writing that much other business. You are doing pretty well as it stands. One step at a time.

NF: Exactly. The biggest stumbling block I see for new agents when they come on is that they try to do everything. My Dad is a specialist. He works only with teachers. He does retirement planning for public school teachers.

That's it. When I first told him that I was looking at getting into the insurance industry, he gave me the best advice. He said, "The people who I have known in this business who have been long-term successful are all people who have picked one niche. They've focused on that and nothing else. The people that I see that never succeed, that are always limping along, are the guys that try and do a little bit of everything."

To that end, I do do some other stuff, but everything I do is complemental to the final expense. I never take my focus off the fact that what I do is sell final expense. I don't take off for AEP. I don't stop selling final expense at any point during the year. If I start feeling like one thing is taking me too far out of my final expense lane, I drop it.

DD: I was in the same position you were in back in 2011, doing research on final expense. I came across John Dugger's posts on the insurance form. He was an inspiration for me. He's part of the reason why I got into this business. I've always kept up with John. For those of you who have never heard of him, John Dugger is a guy who's been in the business at least 10 years, if not longer. He's written $200,000 a year. He started with 15 leads, he's working down to 10 leads now and he writes $200,000. He's a powerhouse and full of a lot of different perspectives on this business. There's one thing that he does that I find interesting that very few others do. I'd like your perspective on this. Several years back he moved to actually delivering policies, rather than having the insurance companies do so. His rationale was that he found that he stumbled across more referrals that way. It gave clients another opportunity to say, "Hey, go see my sister down the street. She needs life insurance."

You run your business in a very similar manner to how John does. Call next day appointments, that kind of approach. Is that something you do, or do you have the insurance carriers deliver the policies? Why do you do it, either way?

NF: I am fortunate to be able to call a JD a good friend of mine. He's been extraordinarily helpful in getting me to where I am. He is a much more organized person than I am. In many ways a much more focused person. I am somewhat envious of how organized and focused he is. I've told him this. I hope that when I grow up I can be like him.

I do deliver a lot of my policies, although not for the same reason that JD does. In Pennsylvania, my main carrier is KSKJ and my secondary carrier is Family Benefit. Family Benefit has wacky rules about delivery. I don't deliver any of their policies. In Pennsylvania KSKJ requires that agents deliver all their policies. So I don't have the choice. I think that we're the only state in the country where they actually require that. It's frustrating because I do write a lot of business with them.

I have got into the habit of delivering, and I'll say, you're not wrong. I don't know that that's the reason why JD delivers. I think that if you asked him, he would tell you that it's not. But you do get a lot of opportunities for additional business and referrals when you deliver.

I don't know if this has to do with delivering myself or not, but my persistency is much higher than the industry average. Not everybody makes that first month's payment, but if they do, I keep 92, 93% of them on the books after month 13. There's a lot of agents that would be happy to be getting 80% persistency for 13 months. Some of that is because I deliver a lot of policies.

I don't deliver them all. Sometimes I end up running out of time. I end up sticking them in the mail with a little note saying, "Hey, I hope you send this delivery receipt back into the company. They would appreciate it." But there is a value there if you can be disciplined and organized enough with your time that you can go and deliver policies yourself. I'm a nerd. I've read dozens of sales books to the point where I don't remember who said what anymore. One of the sales books that I was reading when I very first got into the business touted the concept of high touch selling, where you do develop that relationship. It's better than a 'one and done, get them in and get them out' model.

The way that I've structured my business model, I don't want to spend a lot of time on that initial appointment. However, I do want my clients to think to themselves, "That's the guy that I'm going to. When I have a problem, I'm calling him. When something goes wrong, I'm calling him. When my kids have a problem, I'm calling him." Doing things like delivering policies and helping them to update information on their bank account helps with that. When they want to make a beneficiary change, I go out and I see them. That is stuff that I learned from JD. They're good ways to keep yourself in front of your client. It's more important in terms of rapport building and relationship building than any kind of long extended warm-up that you have at the beginning of your presentation. It develops a genuine relationship.

DD: You've seen many agents come and go. Like we said earlier, this business is boring. There are no secrets here. It's pure 'do what you're told and implement.' You help a lot of guys and interact a lot with different agents. Why do you think most agents fail in this business and what can they do about it to actually succeed?

NF: It is a deceptively difficult business because it is so simple. It's not easy, but it's very simple. There's not a lot of work that you actually have to do. You don't have to come up with anything yourself. You don't need to mess around with fancy sales techniques. You only need to go out and see the people. Buy the leads, set the appointments. Knock on the doors if you're more comfortable with that. But you talk to a lot of agents that are struggling and you ask them, "How many presentations are you giving a week?"

"Oh, I don't know," they'll say, "Five or six."

Well, that's not enough. You ask them, "Hey, are you recording your presentations?"

"I don't want to record a presentation. I don't know how I feel about having a recorder out on the kitchen table while I'm talking to the people."

The best thing that you can do for yourself is to record every presentation that you give and listen to it. Critique yourself. Send it to somebody that you trust to listen to it. Give yourself feedback. You are saying things that you do not intend to say in your presentation.

A lot of agents don't want to commit to a system. It almost doesn't matter what your system is. It's got to be a system that works. There's a lot of systems that work. Pick one and stick to it. You have to. You have to sell out to the line that you're selling. This is true for any kind of insurance. If what you're doing is selling Medicare and what you want to do is be a Medicare agent, you have to sell out. Only sell Medicare. The same is true if you're looking to sell financial planning and annuities. Sell out, just do that. Don't try and mess with other stuff. It's no different in final expense. It's a high volume business. I wrote around 400 policies last year. You write a lot of policies and you cannot write in volume if you're trying to do everything. Pick a thing, pick a path, have a way. Go down that path, stick to it and give it a fair shake. Give yourself hours of blindly following the path before you decide that that path doesn't work.

There are agents out there that are writing $200,000, $250,000 a year. They are regularly and consistently telling you that that is the path that you should take, so believe that. In many ways, this is a counter-intuitive business, especially if you've come from other sales backgrounds. A lot of people who have been in other sales before, in non-insurance, some in insurance, have a hard time adjusting to the fact that this business is about the people, not the product. It's about understanding how those people work and talking to them about things that are meaningful to them. A lot of times people come in, they've done a lot of term life selling, they've done a lot of high-level substantial planning. They want to talk to people about universal life products, guaranteed universal, cash values and buying term and investing the difference.

This is all sorts of crazy stuff that does not matter to our people. Our people send this card in because they are concerned that when they die, their kids are going to be left on the hook with a bill that they can't afford. That's the only thing that matters to 95% of them. I'm talking to them about that in a way that makes sense to them and in a way that builds their trust in me. That's everything. That's hard for a lot of guys. The easiest thing to do is find a mentor, pick a path, follow that path.

DD: You've come from the teaching profession into this. I'm sure you've seen the difference. Sales is such an interesting business and it isn't hard work. There is a lot harder work out there. I find that the biggest obstacle to success in this business is yourself. Self-doubts. It's psychological warfare. It's hard to see that from the outside.

NF: The main obstacle is that you don't have anybody but you out there. It's only you and your own self-doubt. It creeps into your head. It's why I spend so much time doing things like posting on the Facebook forums, stuff like that. It's good to talk to other people that do this. There's nobody else that can understand final expense other than final expense agents. It's its own beast.

It's good to have that support. The one downside to this business is that most agents are completely alone. They don't have an office to go to. They don't have a manager to talk to. There are good points to it, that we don't have to deal with all that. However, camaraderie is the thing that's missing from a lot of agents lives. It's good to talk to people who are doing this with success. They remind you that they can do it, so you can do it. They keep you mentally on the right course.

DD: Last question. I've been asking this of everybody that I have talked to. Where do you see this business in 20 years? Do you see it being exactly the same? Generation X is 30, 40 years old now. Even a few Millennials as they start hitting their 50s, 60s, and 70s. Are they going to respond to direct mail? Are they going to be the same kind of people that we're seeing now? What do you think we're going towards here in the next couple of decades?

NF: I do think so. A lot of cultural stuff goes on with our people. There is a culture of people that buy final expense policies. I will sit down and I will talk to people who are 70 years old. They have stories about the New York Life agent coming by and collecting debit checks from their parents every week when they were kids. Their grandparents did the same. Now they're buying a final expense policy to make sure that their grandkids are taken care of. They want to make sure their kids talk to somebody soon.

That goes back to what I said about certain areas having their own personality. Certain types of people have their own personality. Final expense people are not like upper-middle-class people. They have different expectations and frankly, a different background. They come from a different place where it is what it is. I will talk to many people who want their kids present when they're making this decision. I never have a problem with that. Most of the time their kids are on board with the idea of their parents buying a final expense policy. And those kids, when they're 60 and 70 years old, they're going to want to buy a final expense policy too.

There may be some minor differences. Like I said, people are texting me now. Facebook may become a larger part of things, but the reality is that they will still be filling out lead return cards. You will still be setting appointments, still going out and talking to people. I'd be very surprised if it changed dramatically.

DD: *A lot of people don't understand that final expense is a mass market. It took me a while to get that. It's a lot of people, but you don't see these people in everyday walks of life. Most people don't understand how they think and why they do what they do. It's a crash course lesson. Before I got into final expense, I dealt with an upper-middle-class market. They have a totally different thought process, a totally different cultural experience. Getting involved in this was a learning curve. I had to adapt to what these people think and do. And their children tend to carry on the same value system. I think we'll see, like you've said, exactly the same kind of people. They may be online more than they are sending direct mail off, but I don't think the basics will change. It will be more or less the same types of people that haven't changed in seven, eight years.*

NF: Yes. A lot of revolutions have gone on in culture and technology. It's a different world now than it was in 2011. I love our people. I love working with this client group. It's a fun group to work with. Not everybody likes it. There is something very different and distinct about them. They're not the toughest people you see in everyday walks of life. This is something that's important to them and they pass that value onto their kids. I don't see that burning out anytime soon.

The ULTIMATE Guide To Generating High-Quality Referrals

Interview with Claude Whitacre

About Claude Whitacre

Claude has sold in customers' homes for the last 35 years. He is a sales speaker and the author of six books on selling. The topic of our conversation is how to generate high-quality referrals that buy.

DD: *So Claude, could you talk about how you got started in selling?*

CW: Well, actually I started selling insurance when I was 21. That was 41 years ago, with Monumental Life. It's a small company. I don't even know if it's still in business. I did that for about a year, then I sold vacuum cleaners for the rest of my life.

During that time, it wasn't just that I was selling. A lot of people sell for 40 years. I've talked to a lot of guys that are old pros. They have been selling for 20, 30 years. In other words, that means they've been learning how to sell for 20 years and they've been getting better every year for 20 years. Talking to them has sometimes been a phenomenal education. Those people are phenomenal. A lot of the time, though, I have talked to somebody who's been selling for 20 years, and what I find out is that they sold for six months, then they have been repeating that six months, every six months, for the last 20 years.

There is a learning process. You can get better and better. Even to this day, I'm still buying sales books and reading and studying and testing new ideas. It never gets old.

DD: Like any other skill, you have to apply yourself and commit to the process. I'm seven years in insurance myself, closer to ten in sales. With what I know versus what I knew even two years ago; the perspective that I have changes each and every year. There's some level of growth. When you're looking back seven or ten years and compared it with where you're at now, has your perspective changed as well?

CW: It did change. Dramatically. I have to tell you the good news, for anybody that is listening that's new. The first year or two, that's when you make all your mistakes, all your big dumb mistakes. You make most of those right at the beginning. After a year, you've read a few books on selling, taken a few courses, listened to a good sales manager. Maybe you work with somebody that really knows how to sell and they become your mentor. You try to figure out how to do the business, how to sell. You'll be 90% as good as you're ever going to get in the first year or two. It doesn't take 40 years to learn how to sell. Most of the big objections, most of the big problems in selling, the hurdles, you learn how to overcome in the first two or three years. It takes 40 years because it's all-encompassing. Every once in a while (not very often nowadays) I'll hear something that I haven't heard before. I say to myself, "If I ever hear that again, I need to have an answer."

I read a book by Malcolm Gladwell. It claimed that after 10 years most experts have been doing whatever they've been doing for 10,000 hours. 10 years of three hours a day. After 10,000 hours, pretty much you're an expert. That's also my theory.

DD: Part of sales, of course, is this prospecting. Finding people that are interested in what you have to say and more often than not, buying from us.

One of the best ways, if not the best way to generate high-quality leads that buy is to generate referrals.

That's where I want to start. A lot of agents in my business, a lot of salespeople in general, still cold call. Not that there's anything wrong with that, but we both believe that referral generation is an ideal strategy for the best return on your time. Could you talk a little bit about the advantages of referrals over cold calling?

CW: There's nothing wrong with cold calling. I did it for the first 30 years. After the first few years. I didn't have to cold call. I did it to get new lead sources. That's what I was looking for. Then I could get referrals from those people. That's what I was doing. In the beginning, when I was selling life insurance, I had a sales manager and we would be at the sales meeting. Once a week everybody would talk about their numbers. Since my last name is Whitacre, I went last.

Almost all of the guys were the same. One would say, "Well, I made 150 calls, I had 32 appointments and I had five presentations."

"I made 250 calls," said the next guy. "I had 8 presentations and I made no sales."

They would go around the room like that and then get to me. Now, this wasn't at the beginning, this is after I'd been selling for many months and I had discovered how to do referrals from other salespeople.

"OK, Whitacre, what about you?"

"Well, let me think. I made eight calls, had seven appointments and six sales."

We would do that every week. After about two or three months, because I'm kind of outspoken, I'm not as demure as some people, I said, "Look, guys, nobody's asking me how I'm doing this. So, one of two things is happening: either all of you are lying or you're just incredibly terrible at this. Calling 150 people and nobody's buying? I don't even think that's possible!"

Of course, from then on, they didn't invite me. "Claude," they said, "You don't need to come to any more meetings."

It was because I was working referrals. I had figured it out. I had read a few books on referrals at the time. I talked to a few salespeople that I knew that were selling other things. They told me how they got referrals.

By the way, if you are reading this and thinking 'if you are selling life insurance, why would you switch?', the reason that I switched to vacuum cleaners is that somebody came to my home and showed me a vacuum cleaner. It was shiny. I said "That's cool. I want to sell that." That's all it was. Shiny Objects Syndrome!

One of the things that every new salesman hears is that you need to get referrals. But, in almost all their experiences, the first two or three people asked for referrals say, for example, "I'll tell you what, I can't think of anybody right now, but if I do, I'll give you a call." Or, "I'm kind of busy right now. Call me back in a week and I'll see if I can think of somebody."

You never get referrals. If you do get a referral, it never pans out. It only takes a short time for salespeople to think that this referral thing doesn't work well. It doesn't mean that referrals don't work. It means that the way you are setting up the referrals and the way that you're contacting them is not the right way. You're doing it incorrectly. You're pretty well guaranteeing that the referrals are not going to be coming your way. You're guaranteeing that they're not going to talk to you.

And it's complicated. Cold calling is much simpler. Getting referrals is almost a presentation. It weaves its way through your sales presentation. It's not a three-minute presentation at the end of the sales presentation to get the referrals. There's more to it. In fact, in my book on sales prospecting, a third of my book gives you step by step instructions on how to get referrals, how to contact the referrals, all the verbiage, the whole script. It'll apply to almost any kind of selling too, which is good.

DD: *So why do companies tell you to cold call?*

CW: They don't know how to get the referrals. Companies and managers say to cold call because they don't have to do it. That's exactly why. There's a cold calling script. So they tell you to make those calls. Every insurance company, every sales company, I'm sure, has a script of some sort where you make your call. I remember making cold calls, my second or third day on cold calling, on the phone to complete strangers that have never heard of me. I can almost remember the verbiage now: "I have an idea that I would like to share with you, it's only going to take a few minutes, when is the best time to catch you and your husband home..." And I remember them never, ever, letting me come into their home to talk to them.

With referrals, you've jumped over all the sales resistance hurdles because you're a friend of a friend. Maybe they don't trust you yet, but they trust their friend. They trust their friend's opinion. Giving, and getting, referrals is the most natural thing in the world. A lot of salespeople say that people don't like to refer things. Of course they do. Have you ever talked to a friend of yours about a movie and said, "You should go see that movie, it's a really good movie."? That's a referral. If you say something good about somebody else and that person you're talking about is in business, that's a referral. But there are ways to structure it to make it more efficient.

If you have 100 clients, 100 people that have bought from you, I can't think of a reason why you'd ever have to cold call again. I know for me and for most people that's true. When I first started getting referrals, I did it by going back to the people that I cold called. I started talking to them about referrals. That's how I started my base. The only reason I had to cold call after that was if I was in a different area and thought that I would get more names. My referral lists were wearing down. I thought that I would inject some new people in there. Or I would be training somebody new and I would say "Here's how you cold call." I would go out knocking on doors. I wasn't calling on the phone, I was knocking on doors and I would show somebody how to do that. Then, later, I would show them how to get referrals. Knocking on doors is so much easier to teach. I can do that in an hour. Teaching somebody how to get referrals is going to take longer.

DD: Why don't salespeople, in general, ask for referrals? Is it because it's not necessarily taught or is it because it's a mental barrier that salespeople have to asking?

CW: It's not taught much because, even if you have a sales script for getting referrals from a company, it isn't great at getting referrals. For example, we were given a list of three questions you ask the customer. One would be, "Do you know anybody that would be interested in hearing this?"

'You'll Earn a Fortune!' That was a sales presentation that I remember, almost when I first started selling life insurance back around '78, '77. It was forever ago. I believe that every insurance company bought it. It was a flip chart and a script. Part of it was asking for referrals, but the questions were, for example, "Who do you know that is a plumber?", "Who do you know that's just bought a new home?", "Who do you know...?". That's how they taught you how to get referrals.

Assuming that somebody would sit there for an hour and give you names, you'd end up with this incredibly long list of names of people that almost didn't even know the people that are giving you the referral. I never suggest getting fifty names. I ask for two because it's not that much of an inconvenience to ask for two names. I give them the criteria that I want, they give me two names, I ask questions about those two people and then I go talk to those people. If those two people buy, or at least one of them buys, then I'll go back and ask for more. And if those two people don't buy, I don't ask for more names.

DD: Shouldn't you ask for referrals from those who don't buy?

CW: They have to buy. I don't ask those that don't. This is a tendency, not an absolute rule, but people that buy give you referrals that are good referrals and more referrals that buy. The reason is, when somebody gives you a referral and they didn't buy before you talk to that referral, that person's going to talk to that prospect and what are they going to tell them? They're going to tell them that they didn't buy and they're going to have to give a reason why they didn't buy. They can't say "I'm an idiot. You should buy, but I'm an idiot, so I didn't." They can't give that reason. So they're going to come up with some reason why it's not for them. "I'm going to shop around a little bit more.", something like that.

If you run those referrals, pretty soon these people that you're going to go see, all that they know is that everybody who you talked to didn't buy. What do they think? "I don't know what's wrong with this guy, I don't know what's wrong with this idea that this guy is showing, but I don't want to talk to him when nobody buys from him."

You want to go see somebody that only knows two or three people that you've talked to, but all those people have bought. What do they think now? They think it's expected. It's natural for them to buy as well. It's a form of peer pressure. If I go see somebody and they know five people that I've talked to and they've all bought from me, it's unusual for that person to not buy. It's hard for that person to not buy. You want this web of buyers. It expands, getting bigger and bigger. That's what you want.

You don't want webs of non-buyers. You'll start out with more non-buyers than buyers, but very quickly, if you only see buyers, you're going to end up seeing other people that buy. They know other people have bought from you and so now it's a habit. It's all a group thing. It's tribal. People want to be like their friends. If those other friends didn't buy from you, they want to be like them too. I stopped getting lists of non-buyers. They're the worst.

DD: *What do you actually ask for in the referral portion of the sales call?*

CW: It's not only when you ask for the referral. They know that you are expecting referrals and they know that you get them, that you work by referral. It's one of the first things I say on a presentation, even if it's a cold call. I have done a lot of public speaking over the years. Afterward, people would either fill out a form or I'd make an appointment with them right then and there. I would go see them and one of the first things I'd say is "Normally I work by referral, I'm happy that I met you through this organization / I met you through the speech that I gave / you saw somebody give a speech so you know a little bit about what I do." Even if it's a cold call, you can say that you are glad that you got to talk to them by making a cold call, but as a rule, you work by referrals. I don't keep hammering it because it becomes obvious, but a couple of times during the presentation I say, for example, "You're a plumber. I had this other plumber that was referred to me by his accountant and he had a similar problem." I interject a couple of times that there are referrals going on here. People normally give referrals and so it's all about positioning.

Positioning is the most important thing that I can teach people. It's not about asking for referrals. They're not giving you referrals to benefit you. It's nothing to do with you. The entire reason that they're giving referrals is to benefit the people that you're going to go see. That's who's benefiting. They're not doing us a favor. They're doing their friends a favor by introducing them to you so you can give them the same information that you gave your client. They are sharing this information, like when they tell people about a movie: "You need to go see this movie. It's a great movie."

They'll say, "You need to talk to this guy. He's got some great information for you. See whether you decide to do business with him or not. I mean, I did, but it's up to you. You should talk to this guy. He has something I think that would help you."

You want a position like that. It's not you asking them for referrals. If you ask them for referrals, they're doing you a favor. I wouldn't accept that. If someone tries to say "I want to help you out", I wouldn't even let them. If somebody says "I do like you, I want to help you out by giving you some referrals", I'll tell them that they're not helping me, they're helping the people that they refer me to. I'll say it, and mean it, in a very sincere way. Often they'll accept that, but if they ask a question like "How is that benefitting?" I'll tell them that it's because I'm sharing information. The benefit isn't that they do business with me. The benefit is that I share information with them that will help them. They'll have more information and they can make better decisions.

That's what I say. "You're referring me to your friends so that I can help them with the same information that I gave you. Then, when I go see or when I call that prospect, they've already talked to you." The person who gave the referral has to talk to them first. They have to know I'm going to call them. That's another reason why I only ask for a couple of names. I call the guy back and ask if he has talked to Bob and Sally, for example. Two different people, two different families.

"Yes," he says, "I talked to him."

"Are they willing to talk to me?"

If they are, when I call I'll say, for example, "This is Claude from New York life. I was talking to Bill the other day and he mentioned that he talked to you. I promised Bill that I would take the time to call you and stop by quick and share some information that he thought you would want to see. When's the best time to catch you both at home? Are you both going to be home tomorrow at 5:00?" I say it like that. Now, they're not helping. When I'm calling that prospect, I don't want them to think they're helping me by seeing me. It's nothing to do with me. They're helping their friend, which makes it much harder for them to say no. If they say no to me, they're saying no to the person that referred me to them. It's hard to do because you have to use very specific language to put them in that frame of mind.

Once you see a referral, that referral knows that you're expecting referrals because that's how they saw you. It's much easier to get your referrals from that person. That's how you build this web of people that are connected. They know each other and they all bought. That's what you want.

If they don't buy, be nice, because these are referrals. You have to be nice. Immediately call back the referrer after you talk to them, whether they bought or not. It doesn't make any difference. Call back and let them know what happened and always say nice things.

DD: Agents are going to have mental barriers to asking for referrals in this manner. You've mentioned a couple of objections. I hear other agents that I've trained say the same thing. Won't they look needy by asking?

CW: I understand why they say that. Especially when they're brand new and they're afraid. They're afraid they're going to look unprofessional. Well, here are those who get referrals: Doctors, lawyers, CPAs. Those are who get referrals. Those are who ask for referrals. It's not the needy people. The needy people are afraid to ask. They are afraid of rejection. They're afraid that they're not worthy of referrals.

Salespeople are afraid. They wonder what it is that they have done to deserve referrals. Well, you have shown this man or this family some great information. You acted in a very professional way whether they bought from you or not. Your visit helped them. Now they have more information. You have to see it like that. You're not begging. It's not like that at all. You're helping these people. When a doctor comes to your home to give you medicine, he's not begging to give you medicine, he's doing it to help you. When you're talking to a client or potential client, you know you're doing it to help them. That's not a positioning statement. You have to be thinking that as you're doing it because it all comes through as you're talking. But salespeople will say "If I haven't done anything to deserve referrals, they'll think I needed the money. They'll think, especially if the client has been a client for a while, that I'm playing off their friendship, that I'm taking advantage of them."

This is not the case at all. In fact, this is what I found. Let's say you had a client for a year. You read this interview or the third of my book that talks about referrals. You decide to go back and talk to those people that already bought, that you did not get referrals from before. This is what has happened in that year, six months or however long it's been since they bought from you. Believe me, you are a topic of several kinds of their conversations. That client has done one of two things when they talk to other people about you. Either they are complaining because you did something wrong or they're bragging to their friends about what a great decision they made. You want to find out which they have been doing. If they're complaining, first of all, you don't want to go see those referrals. You can fix your client's problems with you, but you can't fix the stories he's already been telling. You can only fix whatever the problem is with your client and thank them. They'll even want to say "Why don't I give you some referrals? Why don't I send you to see Bob?"

You ask "Did you already talk to Bob?"

"Oh yes," they say. "But it's OK. I'll tell him..."

You don't want to do that. Now the guy's told some story. It's probably not even true, but they've told some story about you that's made you look bad. You don't want that aggravation.

However, usually what happens is that they were bragging, "Oh, I got this new prep plan. It's great. I had this other plan, This is a brand new one. It's great. I feel so secure. And I think I got a great deal. My guy takes care of me."

The people that they brag to, those are the people you want to go see. Those people are preconditioned to buy. It's going to be really hard for those people not to buy after their friend bragged about how great you are. To that prospect, you're a celebrity. You're not a pest, calling them to bother them. You're a celebrity. That other guy was bragging about knowing you, about buying from you, about what you sold. He thinks that you're the greatest thing since sliced bread. When you call these people, not only do they take your call, but they would like to know more about your program. You're not getting "Well, OK, as long as it only takes five minutes." You're getting "I want to know more about that."

That's what you do. Go back and find all the people that you've talked to before. Don't call the people that didn't buy, call the ones that bought. Find the ones that bragged about buying and then you ask "Who did you talk to?" That's my favorite question.

"Since you bought it, did you tell anyone about it? Who did you talk to about this?"

"I told my brother Harry and three guys at work."

"What did you tell them?"

They don't know that question is coming, and it's easier to tell the truth, so they will either tell you or they'll hedge. If they say that they don't really remember what they said, that means that they said something bad. Usually, they'll say, for example, "I told them that you were very good and it's a good program."

"And what did they say?"

"Well, they said that if you're ever in the neighborhood or if you ever called them, they'd probably talk to you."

That comes up, you're not going to believe how often that comes up. There are potential clients waiting, but your client doesn't know to call you to ask you to go see them.

Then you go see brother Harry. That's one of the ways you get these great referrals that are almost guaranteed to buy from you. They're guaranteed to see you, and they're almost guaranteed to buy. Keep the conversation limited to only a few people. If those people buy, go back and get more names. It doesn't happen very often, but when I was selling vacuum cleaners, I had a few that I went back and back and back to after the first three referrals. One woman gave me around 45 and 44 of them bought. Another one gave me around 42 and 40 of them bought. You get these trees and you only need a few of those. Then you're off to the races. You're not doing anything else. Once you get good at referrals, you don't want to do anything else. This becomes your business.

DD: I can hear agents and salespeople reading this and saying "Yes, this is what happens when everything works perfectly. What if I ask them for referrals and they shrug it off? Even if they buy? They tell me that they can't think of anybody. They ask to follow up with me later." I know we've all experienced that. How do you deal with that?

CW: If they say they can't think of anybody, it's because you asked the wrong question. Don't ask them something like "Who do you know that I could talk to?" Now they've got the whole freaking world to think about. They have to try to remember every person they've ever met, and that is a huge job for them. You're asking a huge favor. You want to narrow it down to almost nobody.

When I get referrals, I find the best people to talk to by giving usually two or three qualifications as the main qualifications. Say you're selling, for example, a social security supplementation, Medicare, something from a case. You might want to see people of a certain age. Maybe you want them to be married, maybe you want them to be single. You might want them to be homeowners. If you've been in sales for more than a year or two, you know the kind of people that are more likely to buy. You'll mention a type of a job or a type of income or if they're in business, a type of a business. You narrow it down. When I was selling vacuum cleaners, I would say that I worked by referral and I'd like to see married couples over the age of 25, that are homeowners, that have carpet, that have pets and have talked to a salesman before.

That last is the qualification you should always have. It doesn't matter what they have bought before. You want to talk to people that have bought. Say your job is going to people's homes, that's how you talk to people and make appointments. You want to talk to people that let people in their homes.

DD: That's a good point. There's a lot of people out there that would meet every other criterion that have the 'do not solicit' signs up.

CW: There is. I did a study, using my own personal business, of the percentage of the population that bought from us or that was likely to buy from us. I'm talking about adults that lived in a home and had jobs. Of those people, 6% were going to buy. 6%. If I was a great salesman and I could close everybody, I would sell 6%. I figured out that I won't go see the other 94%. I'll only see the 6%. In every population, you can live off of that 6% very well. You'll never run out of those people meeting one of the criteria. I've found so in selling vacuum cleaners, you'll see the same thing in selling life insurance. Some of your listeners might think that it's different, but it's not; buyers are buyers. Somebody lets you in your home and buys, they are far more likely to let somebody else come in their home and they're far likelier to buy. Why? Because they're in the habit of doing that. I happen to be part of the 94% that don't buy. I don't let people in my home and I don't buy. It's hard to get me on the phone. It's impossible to come to my home. There are some people that have mental hurdles. They don't want somebody to come to their home for whatever reason. They don't buy. They're used to not buying.

However, there are people that will buy. My parents bought everything. Every single thing. Anybody came to the door, they let them in and they bought. I do not remember, growing up, them ever not buying something. It's not because they're dumb. It's not because you're taking advantage of them. One of the first things I always ask when I go into somebody's home is "Has anybody ever been to your home to show you something?" It doesn't make any difference what it is you are presenting; your product or service, "Has that ever happened?"

"Yes."

"What was it?"

They will tell me. Now that I know those people are in the habit of letting somebody in their home and buying, I will compliment them on their purchase, no matter what. They're far more likely to buy from me if they've bought from the other guy. It has nothing to do with how good I am or how good he is. They're simply far more likely to buy.

If somebody buys, I ask him if anybody has ever been to their home before and what happened. I don't say "Tell me, were they nice people?" I wonder what happened. I do it in a very ambiguous way. I don't want to feed them what they tell me. I want them to tell me whatever they really think. They'll tell me either their tale of woe or they'll tell me what a great thing it was and they'll brag about making the purchase. I don't know if it's true or not. All I care about is their attitude. I want to know how they think, how they saw it, if they liked the guy, if they didn't like the guy and if they made a purchase.

If they made a purchase, I always tell them that it was a good purchase and here's why. The worst thing you can do if you're in somebody's home or if you're talking to a prospect is telling them that a previous purchase was a bad idea. It doesn't make any difference what it is. Even if they tell you that it was a bad idea. "That was so dumb," they might say, "I shouldn't have bought that boat."

"I don't know," I'll say, "I would have. It sounds like you made a good decision. It sounds like you thought about it and made a great decision." Why? Because you are telling them that their previous decision to buy was a good one and they're hearing it. They're not consciously thinking this, but their brain is processing this idea that buying is good.

If you tell them that a previous buying decision was a mistake, even if they tell you it was a mistake and you agree with them, what are they going to do? They're thinking, "Well, I made that mistake before, but I'm not going to make that mistake again. I'm not going to buy from you." If you insult a previous buying decision, the only way they can get even with you is by not buying. And they'll kill the sale. You have to tell them what a great decision they made. It doesn't make any difference if it's insurance. It doesn't make any difference what they know, what they bought, it's the fact that they bought.

DD: It's that behavior pattern. We want to repeat that behavior pattern.

CW: Yes, We want to help them with that behavioral pattern. I want to know if they give referrals before I want to know what happened. I want to know the details so that I can help them. If they have good feelings about it, I want to give them better feelings about it. If they have bad feelings about it, for example, "I gave referrals before and he screwed me over and he was terrible! I never saw them and I'm never going to give referrals again! I learned my lesson," I want to zero it out and make it so it's not so bad, but I probably wouldn't ask them for referrals. At that point, if you're great at this and you want to take a half an hour, you can slowly wheel them back around to zero. Then the dialogue will go the other way. Now they're your friend. You can do that if you want. I don't spend the time doing that. If they're a negative, I don't try to turn them into a positive. I want to find the positive people.

DD: You're looking for your guy, as they say. the one that makes it worth it.

CW: I'm looking for my guy. Even when I was cold calling, knocking on doors, after a while my whole idea was this. I would knock on doors and all I cared about was getting one nice guy. That's all I wanted. At the end of the day, I'm looking for that nice guy. The one that'll be nice whether he buys or not. A nice guy who'll talk to me. He might offer me a cup of coffee. I'll sit there and talk to them for awhile. He's pleasant and I'm pleasant and that's it. That's all I care about. I don't want to talk to everybody. Not everybody can buy and seeing them all will kill you if you're a salesman. I was talking to everybody and I was only closing one out of 20. It was terrible. Because I was seeing everybody, I didn't care who I talked to. I was trying to sell a vacuum cleaner to somebody that bought one yesterday. I was trying to sell vacuum cleaners to somebody without floors. I was talking to somebody that's unemployed. I talked to anybody.

DD: *Are you saying that not everybody's a prospect?*

CW: I am saying that. Not only is not everybody a prospect, there are grades of prospects. What you want to do, in my book, is to see the people most likely to buy. You find out who those people are and then you concentrate on them. It's not even a socioeconomic group. It's people that have bought from you before. People who know other people that buy from you. That also becomes a great qualifier. They know five people that bought from you. They're going to buy or at least be nice to you as long as you're nice to them, of course. You can screw it up!

DD: *In the insurance business, like in any business, 90% of agents flunk out in the first year. Maybe it's because they sell in this manner, where everybody is a prospect. They need to figure out who the qualified prospects that meet the best criteria for buying are. Typically those are the easiest. We all want to deal with the people are the easiest to deal with. It makes life easier and these methods allow for that.*

CW: Yes. There's plenty of low hanging fruit. The problem is that new people can't do this. When I was training new people, the first thing I would do is send them on cold calls. I needed to train them how to do cold calls before I trained them on how to do referrals. They had to have a little bit of experience. I wanted them to go out there. I don't want to say it in a mean way, but they needed to get their nose bloodied a little bit, have a few rejections. They needed to know what was going to happen. But I also wanted to make sure that they saw sales, so I would take them with me. I didn't give them the sale, they came with me to see me work. I wanted them to see that people bought. I wanted them to see that it was natural for people to give me money. It was natural for people to buy. It was expected that they were going to buy. That was an important thing for me to do with the new guys.

Part of it is that new people think they can't sell. I can solve that problem by teaching them how to sell. I can't solve the problem of people that aren't going to buy. I can convince new people that they can sell. I can't convince them that people are going to buy. I have to show them that there are people that buy. They have to see that. I want them to see that people do buy, three or four or five times, in the beginning.

They should even see the ones that don't buy. When somebody is new, the worst thing that can happen is that the client is going to say no. Well, you had that before you talked to them. It's not like you go into their home and they either buy or they punch you in the nose. Once, I had a new salesman, a brand new guy. He asked me "What do you do if they reach over and try to choke you?"

"What did you do to them that they want to do that?" I asked, "What did you do?"

When I was doing in-home vacuum cleaner sales, I had 7,200 customers that bought from me. That doesn't include insurance buyers. I only started counting when I started selling vacuum cleaners. 7,200 sales and around 12,000 presentations, to the nearest 100. I don't know how many doors I knocked on. Around 50,000. That's a lot of sales. And in my entire life, I've only had two people ask me to leave. Both of those assignments were my fault. I said something embarrassing or I said something derogatory or some horrible thing. I said something once, early in my career, I won't tell you what, because it's bad. The guy's eyes got really big.

"You're not going to let that go, are you?" I said.

"Nope."

"I'll just gather my things."

And that's funny, that one time. It makes for a good story. One time in 35 years of home sales.

DD: *Our new rep is learning your method. They're applying it and, my gosh, they've actually got somebody giving them a name that meets certain criteria. They're excited. They say "You should call my brother." What happens after that? What should they do?*

CW: Well, first of all, you want to know why. The quick answer is they need to ask them questions about their brother and his situation. Just because this guy wants me to call his brother doesn't mean his brother's a good prospect. What kind of work does he do? Is he married? Where does he live? Roughly how old is he? If you sell insurance, ask if he knows anything about his insurance. If it's vacuum cleaners, does he know what kind of vacuum cleaner he has? That kind of thing.

Then I would say, "Would you do me a great favor? When I call your brother, he's not going to know who I am and if he's like me, I get a lot of calls, I might say I'm not interested. He might say that. What I'd like you to do is call him and ask him if it's OK if I give him a call." I say it like that. I don't ask him to call his brother and ask him if he'll buy. I don't say "I want you to call him and ask him if I can come over and talk to him." No. I say "I want you to call him and ask him if it's OK if I give him a call."

The reason I say it like that? It's a smaller request. It's easier for the brother to say yes to that. And when he says "Yes, it's OK for him to call," that almost never means "Yes, It's OK for him to call, but I'm not going to talk to him. It's OK for him to call, but that's it. He can only call. I'm not going to do anything else."

This is another reason I'll ask for only a couple of names. I can ask the brother to call right there. If I only have a couple of names, I can say "Could you give him a call right now? Ask him if it's OK if I talked to him?" And he'll call. I have a very small script I give them: You should tell him that he doesn't have to buy anything. This is information that you think he should have and that you think that it would help him if I stop by to talk to him. When he does that, even if he goes completely off script, it doesn't make any difference because it's his brother.

Sometimes, the guy is completely screwing up, and I'll say "Is it OK if I talk to this guy?" It depends on the situation. I don't always do it. I could grab the phone and say "Hi, this is Claude Whitacre. I'm here talking to your brother. We've been having a good time. We've been talking about financial information and he seems to think that I should talk to you. That I can help you. I promised him that I would. When would be a good time for me to stop by for a few minutes?" It's really hard to say no to those things.

I don't mind that they want to say no on the phone. I'm a stranger that their brother has sent. He's sticking me on them and I understand that. I know that going in, but I want them to say yes because, believe me, they're going to call the brother before I get there.

"What does this guy want?"

"This guy? Oh yes, he's a really nice guy. He's funny and he does have some information that you might like."

"Did you buy?"

"Yes, I bought. I don't know if you want to buy from him, but he has a good program. It's the best I've seen."

Like that, they half sell it for you. It's half sold before you get there. When I was selling vacuum cleaners in people's homes, I would even want him to give the price. Get it all out there.

"Well, how much is it?"

"It's $2,000."

"Damn, you paid all that for a vacuum cleaner?"

"Yep. You should see it. You don't have to buy it, but you should see it."

By the time I get there, this guy is actually considering it. "Should I buy a $2,000 vacuum cleaner or shouldn't I?" He's already considering it and that's almost insane! Why in the world would somebody consider that? When I get there, all I have to do now is show them good value. All I have to do now is what I did before. Halfway through the presentation, they're saying "Wow! I thought my brother was nuts but this is a great thing." Show the program because the client is not going to have explained the whole insurance program. He can't remember the whole program, but he'll have told them a couple of highlights by the time you get there. Show them this, then show them other things, "You also get this and this and this and this."

"Wow. I didn't even know that. Wow. My brother told me it was this much a month or this much a year. I didn't know he got this, is this exactly what my brother got?"

If it is, tell him yes. If it isn't, say "No. You know why? Because you're not your brother. Your brother's a different situation to you. Not the same age that you are, he has different needs to you."

DD: It's interesting listening to the referral strategy because, in my mind, a lot of it goes back to salespeople with low self-esteem. They don't realize or appreciate the value that they deliver to their clients and the kind of people that they can help. I had a phone call with a guy in the final expense business. He's a multimillion-dollar agent, he's been around for years. As I'm listening to you teach these concepts, I'm thinking that this is exactly what this guy did. He's a top-tier recruiter and he peppered into his presentation "People refer business to me. That's all I do. I know this guy from this company and I've known him for years." He named names, people I've heard of. "People like to help me. They want to work with me." It wasn't over the top, but as I left the phone call, I'm thinking, "I wonder if he's talked to so and so in Florida? I could have him talk to this guy in Texas." I've already gone through this in my mind. I'm not doing any kind of business with this guy, but I didn't hang up the phone. I started immediately thinking of people. He impressed upon me the same teaching

that you're doing here, which is this is how we do business. And it's funny how you lead the way. It's kind of a self-fulfilling prophecy.

CW: Are you going to ask me about my 'follow the salesman' deal?

DD: Yes, this is my favorite part. Why don't you explain the concept to us and elaborate?

CW: This was around 30 years ago. I've been asking for referrals before, working referrals for a long time, selling vacuum cleaners. I'm in a home, they bought from me and I'm asking them for referrals. They're giving me referrals and they let slip that someone had been in the home, selling, before. This was before I even knew to ask if they ever bought anything from anybody else, they just let it slip. They said, "This is like that water filtration system that we bought."

"What do you mean?" I asked.

"Well, this guy came to our home and for $4,000 we bought a water purification system."

"You bought the water purification system?" At the time I was selling a vacuum cleaner for around $1000.

"Yes, and he asked for referrals."

"He asked for referrals?"

Well, once a decade, a brilliant idea pops into my head, and this was it. It popped into my head. "So you gave him referrals?" I ask.

"Yes."

"Do you know the people that he went to see?" I asked. "Do you know who bought and who didn't?"

"Yes."

"Could you give me the referrals that bought?"

"Sure!"

And they gave me the names of people that bought. Now, what do I have? I have the name and addresses of people that I know a lot about because I'm asking qualifying questions. I don't waste my time and their time. I want to make sure that at least they have the ability to buy from me if they want to. I don't want to see somebody that has no ability to buy. I don't want to see anybody that has no need for my product, so I'm not going to hit the button to buy. What I have now are prospects who are used to having somebody call them on the phone. They are used to having them come over to their home, used to them showing them something very expensive. They are used to buying from them that day and giving them money and then giving them referrals. They're already trained. These customers are already trained in everything you want them to do.

This is what happened. If I remember correctly, they bought the water purification system at least a year, maybe two, before I got there. Now I'm following that salesman, that's what I'm doing. I'm going to go see all the people that he sold to and I'm getting referrals from those people for other people that he sold to. Here's what's happening. I'm catching up to him. Pretty soon, I'm seeing the people that bought from him nine months ago, six months ago, three months ago. Why? Because I'm not going to see all the people that he didn't sell to. I'm not going to see the people who said no to him. I'm only seeing the people that said yes.

Eventually, I caught up. I never met this guy. It was one salesman and I caught up with him. I couldn't go any further. And what happened after I stopped seeing those water purifying system customers? Well, I figured out before I ever got to that point that I wanted to ask, for example, what about the fire alarms? What about the swimming pool that they bought? There are other things that they bought. I would go see those strings of referrals too. I kept branching off into other strings of referrals. I didn't have to stop after I saw all the people about the water purifier.

Your clients, your students, and your listeners sell insurance. Well, this happened in the opposite way to me. I was followed. I'd been selling vacuum cleaners for many years. A friend of mine, his name was Dave, got an insurance business and he asks "Can you refer anybody to me?" I already knew the system. I was used to going to see people that are buyers. "Who should I go see?" he asks.

I said, "I'll tell you who you should go see. This lovely couple. They're younger, here's their phone number. They liked me. Tell them that I suggested that you call them and I suggested that they should talk to you."

It's been too long, I don't remember if I called them ahead of time to pave the way for this guy or if he just went to see them. But, he went to see them and he starts racking up a lot of sales because he's going to see the people that bought from me. He's going to see buyers. I remember then going into a home, I'm showing my vacuum cleaner and I get done. They said, "You know, we probably would go ahead and buy this, but a couple of days ago we bought this great expensive insurance program, like $100 a month from this guy named Dave."

"What's his last name?" I asked. They told me. "Oh no!" I say, "He caught up to me already!"

That's what happened. I didn't get mad. I thought it was funny. Oh my gosh, he really made that work! I was very proud of him for doing that. He saw people that are used to buying. Don't go see people that have never bought. Go see people are used to buying in the way that you sell. That's one of the best ways.

DD: Did you use any other methods to find people that bought?

CW: I would go to other vacuum cleaner companies and I would say "I'll pay you for your list of names of buyers that already bought from you. I'll service them, for no charge. I don't charge it for this at all. I'll go out and ask if they need anything or if they need service on the vacuum cleaners that you sold."

"You do that," they would say. "Go see these people." They didn't like to do service. The companies don't like to go back over and over and over again to do service. They want to sell, they don't want to do service.

I go back and call them up. I call people who bought five years ago from them because I know this: the average length of time between buying new vacuum cleaners is about five years. I'd go see people about a vacuum cleaner bought for a lot of money five years ago and now I'm going to show them something different. They're probably going to buy from me, and they do. Then that would become another string of referrals. I didn't need to cold call anytime. You don't have to that.

I was a distributor for selling vacuum cleaners. People in my company, they knew who I was and they would want to work with me. They would say "I want to find out what you do!" And I would tell them that I work referrals. They were still used to working, going to the fair and getting leads that way. They made cold calls on the phone and offered gifts if they could come out and talk to clients. A lady that worked with me for a week, she says "I figured out the difference between you and me."

"Well, what's that?" I asked.

She says "Well, I'll go out, I'll do 10 presentations in a week, sell two. And I'll think, gee, that's pretty good. I made two sales. You'll go out and do six presentations in a week, sell five and agonize over that sixth one!"

That's true, I guess!

I can teach you how to close better, I've noticed over the decades that I can increase my closing percentage. But it's by small amounts. Whereas seeing better quality prospects can multiply the sales. It doesn't just add another 10%, it can double and triple sales. Almost all the big breakthroughs I've had where I've started selling tons more are in the way I got the leads in. What I said when I got the leads, how I handled the introductions, how I got people to introduce me to somebody else. That was the part that gave me the most profit.

Also, it's more fun seeing referrals. Everybody likes to talk to you. They want to talk to you. You're not bothering people. You're not a pest, you're a welcome guest. People are looking forward to you stopping by. That's a completely different experience to what a lot of salespeople are used to. It's somebody saying "Oh yes, come on in. You are a guest!" rather than "All right. I'll talk to you, but I'm not promising anything!" You don't want to hear that. You want to hear "Yes, please, come on in. I have a couple of questions for you." You answer the questions and it becomes more of a conversation. Not a hard pitch. It sounds more like a conversation at that point.

DD: Claude, I want to thank you so much for joining me today. Everybody reading this is going to be thrilled with the amount of information that you've given out. How can my audience find out more about your sales training books and the services they offer?

CW: Just go to www.amazon.com. Type in Claude Whitacre, and you'll pull up my books. I have six of them, with a couple on the way. There's two that they should buy. One is called 'Sales Prospecting' by Claude Whitacre. That's the book that we have been discussing a little bit about.

I also have one about one call closing. Those are the two books of those six that they should read. The sales prospecting one probably is the one that generates more income for salespeople.

DD: Claude, you're just wonderful for sharing all this information. I'm going to be putting it to use immediately and know my audience is. Thank you so much for talking to us.

How To Sell Annuities Without Purchasing Leads

Interview with Stephen Burgess

About Stephen Burgess

Stephen Burgess is the Head Annuity Trainer for American Senior Advocates, and has been licensed as a life and health insurance agent since 2010.

DD: Steve, let's start by discussing how you generate your annuity leads. It's a bit unique.

SB: I use a dialer called Mojo. It's a state-of-the-art dialer setup for sales agents. It's called a 'live line' dialer. As soon as the person picks up, it goes through a cell phone instead of a computer. As soon as they answer the phone, they are on my headset.

So here is my day: I cold call over the phone for an hour between 8:45 to 10:00 am. I organize myself, I figure out the ZIP code I'm going to, then turn on my dialer. In my dialer are people from age 63 to 75 that have been narrowed down to the exact type of people I'm looking to talk to. They make a little over $15,000 a year, but they don't make more than about $50,000 a year. I look for that window of income where they'll have between $20,000 to

$180,000 in investments (retirement funds) and own a house. I prefer prospects who own their property over prospects who rent.

I work a ZIP code and book appointments for the next day. Here's how the calls sound:

"Hi, Mrs. Jones. My name is Stephen Burgess. I'm with the senior advocate program here in Volusia County. I work closely with Volusia County residents who are over the age of 63. The purpose of my call is to make sure that you are aware of all the new federal and state private programs that could be of benefit to you. I also deliver a catalog of county senior services and their contact information.

"The main purpose of this call is that I am scheduled to be in Port Orange on Wednesday and Thursday of this week. I hope I can stop by, introduce myself and share that information with you. I have 10:15 am available, early morning, or would 2:45 pm work better for your schedule?"

I present my Florida credentials at the time of the meeting. If they book the appointment, I log it in my calendar. I like to run four or five appointments a day.

The following day, I meet the people with whom I had talked. I have notes on them. I have looked at their houses. I know that they are within 10 to 15 minutes of each other. It's a very organized day. If I have a space in between, I know I'm going to have lunch at 1:00 pm.

If I have people that I tried to see in that area and I haven't seen before, I always have a backup plan. There are a couple of things that I do. That's the difference between doing annuity business, which is directed via a cold call, as opposed to final expense business, which have clients responding directly for insurance. The closing ratios and the type of business are substantially different. I have the opportunity on any account to go anywhere from a small Medicare supplement plan to a final expense plan. I could move legacy of $200,000 and make $15,000 on the sale. The spectrum of where my income comes from on any one visit is vast.

The process of working on the client is very similar to final expense. You start on a broad highway. You look around the house and make compliments. I like to find people who are family oriented. Family pictures are the best indication of that. I see those, I know there is legacy there. Somebody is moving money in order to take care of their kids. I slowly narrow down from the meet and greet. If they offer a cup of coffee, I always accept it. It's a little dangerous because you get too much caffeine, but I accept hospitality because it creates a favorable ambiance.

The first thing that I do with people, before I ever go into my factfinder, is get credibility. I start off by providing information such as what the county offers in terms of senior contact information. All you have to do is go to Google and search senior services for that county. It will either be a council on aging or other organized senior services in that county. I provide them with the Social Security information (which can be picked up for free from the Department of Social Security) that teaches you how to get online and set up your own account.

Then I explain who I am and what I'm all about. I've told them on the phone that I'm licensed and have credentials. I show them my Florida insurance license and that I am regulated by the Department of Financial Services. I explain I've been background checked and fingerprinted (it's mandatory in the state of Florida that you go through these requirements in order to visit seniors). I also have continuing education that focuses on the needs of people over the age of 63. I am usually helpful, but if I am not, they can kick me out in about 10-15 minutes. Always crack a joke, make it very jovial. I tell them that I would like to gather a little bit of information if it's alright with them. It helps me stay organized. I ask their permission to write down a few notes. That's my fact finder. It starts with a thing called a 'needs analysis'. On the front, it has a circle with four different areas. I start with health insurance, making sure that they have the appropriate health coverage for the county. Do they have wills, trusts, long-term care and financial planning in place? Those are the four circles.

DD: My next question is about the Confidential Needs Analysis. This is a completely different setup to that which we use in final expense, mortgage protection, or any kind of one product approach. How does it work when you're in the process of working with the client? What is the intent of doing a fact finder, as opposed to asking for the annuity business, if that's what you're going for upfront?

SB: The way you get to annuity sales opportunities is through credibility and service. That's the prize at the end of doing the job correctly. I inform the clients of the services that are in the county. Before I get to the point where I'm selling them something, I'm going to be of service first. The purpose of the fact finder is laid out to be of service in an order. I start with where they are, how old they are, if they've been married before. If they are divorced you try to be helpful. Were they married for over 10 years? You're trying to make sure their Social Security is maximized. You ask them if they have any kids, if they have to travel to meet the kids. The reason you ask that question is to find out if they are on a PPO plan or an HMO plan. If they have to travel all over the country on an HMO plan, then they have a problem. When they visit their kids they are going to have an issue with their carriers.

The next question I ask is particularly for people over the age of 63. I go through their health coverage. Here's my first chance to find out if I have a client with whom I can work. I ask them, "What card do you show when you go to a doctor?" If they go get their Social Security card and their health coverage card, I now have them doing what I want them to do. I want them to understand that I can be of service. I can make a recommendation. I'm not interested in selling them health insurance. I really think that is a detriment. I can sell them a Medicare supplement if they have too much money, but if they are on health insurance, I make recommendations about what works best in the county.

Here is the next part where the fact finder really works. You ask them about their health. I'm asking them the same health questions that I'm going to find in final expense opportunities when I get to the pivot. I'm gathering that information so that I know what I have before I ever get there. Most of the things are set up to gather the information before you get to the question.

After dealing with health, I move to the next area: Long-term care policies. I ask them if they have any in place. If they don't, then I pull out a sheet called the 'Medicare Spend Down Law'. In that part of the fact finder, I explain to them what Medicare is and how long it lasts. I explain when you should go off Medicare, when to go into long-term care, and when that starts draining your account; taking your legacy, your money, and sending it to the nursing home. I tell them that there is a Medicare spend down law to which they can attach the house, the car, the furniture and pay the funeral expenses. They can go after cash value and insurance policies, which leads me to my next pivot.

I'm telling them now that annuities are being protected as opposed to being exposed. In the first two areas of the fact finder, I've set things up psychologically and made the person feel very comfortable. My next pivot is whether he is still paying on life insurance policies or not. If he is, I ask for face value and I try to dive into it. If he is not, then I do the assumptive close; "Is that because those policies are paid up or that you don't have any in place?'

I assume that they have paid up their policy. If they have paid up then that's an asset in the show. If there is no policy in place, that's business I can do. I've learned their health, I've learned that they don't have life insurance in place. I'm ready to go to the next question; "Do you have any paid up funeral expense coverage? Have you thought about it? Have you gone down that road?" Ultimately, where I can be of value to seniors is if they have a will or living trust in place.

At this point, I've gone through the fact finder. I'm about seven minutes into the conversation (although I have a tendency to talk too much. I'm probably 15 minutes into the conversation!). Now I start asking about their finances. I say, "If you don't mind me asking, I have a few questions about your finances. There are certain programs that will be available to you. How much Social Security do you get? Is there a pension? Is the house paid for?" They show me their annuities, stocks, bonds, real estate investments.

Then the final three questions are:

"Is there anything that I can help you with?",

"Do you have a financial planner or somebody that assists you?",

"What can we do today?"

I have gathered all my information. I fold it over and I'm ready to do a presentation or a recommendation where I find a need. That's how I work the fact finder.

DD: Let's talk about how to book appointments. You believe that the best way to market for an annuity is to have the agent book the appointment himself. In your business, you follow exactly the same procedures. You book all of your own appointments. Why do you think that this aspect of the sales process is important?

SB: There are two areas that I find important. First, I like to be extremely comfortable when I get into the car. I like to know exactly what I'm going in for and that's possible if I've booked my own appointments. There is no ambiguity or nervousness. There are certain appointments (I can tell from the call) that will be fun and energetic. If there is a negative energy then I can sense it.

The other area is the continuity from sale to end. Yes, a person can walk in cold on an appointment. But it's better if the conversation is comfortable from step one, which is the meet and greet on the phone. From there to the meet and greet at the house, to the meet and greet at the table, to the gathering of information. All of that slowly narrows it down to focusing on the sale. That process works really well for me. I'm an extremely friendly person on the phone and I take the same tone at the house. I want people to know that when I show up, I'm the same person that they talked to initially.

DD: How do you keep your work organized when you're booking appointments?

SB: That's the beauty of the dialer. It organizes your data. I created my system through trial and failure. There are a lot of people out there selling info. Dave, you actually gave me the best contact. You told me that ListShack.com is a great company. They're very affordable. It's a $50 a month. They give you a $10 trial coupon. What they offer you is downloading as many leads as you want in the area code or zip code.

I'll give you an example. For some reason, I have an appointment out and away, maybe a delayed appointment with a client that I wrote a year ago. I have to go review a policy. I'll pull up fresh data and book two appointments clustered around that one appointment. I'll do one either side, or two after. I don't waste the drive. It only takes me about a half an hour to get on the dialer. It's very efficient as it dials three lines at a time. It is dialing the exact people that I want. It puts them on my headset about every 45 seconds.

The quality of your day starts with booking appointments. If you get good at getting in front of people, you could be mediocre yet be very successful in doing what I do.

DD: *A lot of people think that they will be lucky to get one appointment an hour. There is a lot of rejection that anybody cold calling has to deal with. What's your approach to handling a question like that from an agent? How much time does it take and how do you overcome that? What is the method you use?*

SB: That's a significant question. All the resistance is from people thinking that you are selling something over the phone. I'm not selling anything over the phone. I'm informing them of a beneficial service. I'll give you a typical phone call. I always ask them their names first. If that person doesn't want to talk to me, if they have any kind of resistance whatsoever, they will say they are not interested. It gives them a chance to respond. If they give me their name and greet me, I will greet them right back. Then I go into my spiel, as I mentioned at the beginning of this interview. I do the assumptive close at the end; "Would 10.30am be better for you, or 2.00pm?"

One out of eight people that you'll talk to will book an appointment if you are, like me, dialing 100 people an hour. The idea of doing four appointments in a casual, quick, friendly, informational close is not nearly as difficult as trying to sell the product over the phone.

DD: *How do you handle training new agents to annuity sales?*

SB: I highly recommend that before you dive completely into annuity, you get full training.

We get everybody on the phone at 8:30 am. I'm going to start dialing my prime time for booking appointments with seniors. This is the best time of the day; 8:45 am to 10:00 am. We review how we did.

The other thing is that dialing by myself on the phone is boring and mundane. If I have agents in my headset, I'm talking about it whilst I'm waiting for somebody to pick up. Everybody's muted. Then, all of a sudden I'm back to doing the appointment. Sometimes there is some banter - a little game of tennis - going on between me and the appointment. I play the game of tennis and I get it back down to where I want to do it. Now I have the appointment. I stop and unmute everybody. We talk about what happened and how it worked.

There are a lot of different things that you're going to go up against. You start getting too many techniques that happened on the fly. They happen over and over again. If you're live with somebody who has been doing it an awful long time, they can explain why certain things happened and those techniques were used. Then these agents listening in, they've seen and heard about everything that they are going to come up against. They'll have the confidence in their voice to book the appointment.

DD: *It seems to me that there would be potential resistance to asking your annuity prospects questions about personal finances. Do you find that there is much resistance towards that? How do you overcome that potential objection?*

SB: The first thing to say about resistance is that it is a good sign. People who are overly forthcoming with information generally have no information to give. If you get to the point where you ask about money and they have no money, they have no problem telling you that. If a person is giving you resistance, it's good news.

Don't push too hard. You can always pivot and come back. If you get to a point where you're asking about Social Security, you say that you want to make sure that they qualify for all the benefits that you have. If they are at a certain level of Social Security and have a pension, you can help them check that the numbers are correct. That's the only reason for the question. Resistance is a good thing. Yesterday, I met a lady that started off with, "I'm not doing anything with my money." 45 minutes later, she was $55,000 in annuity that was being signed and moved. It's a matter of being credible from the beginning.

Let them realize that you're different. There are a lot of different ways to do that. Which you use depends on the client. If it's an intelligent client who is with a financial planner and there's a lot of money involved, I tell them, "I focus all my attention on one area, 401K, IRAs, and annuities. Do you have those products?" That takes away the conflict that the prospect has. He doesn't want me looking at his stocks, bonds or investments and I'm not interested in those. I'm interested in his retirement money. I go back to the money that they have put away while they were working from day one. I try to get an emotional bond with the money. When you do that with people over the age of 65, even if they have a lot of money, they understand what you're there for and the fact that you have some expertise in that area. I always use the phrase, "Could I get a fresh set of eyes on it to make sure everything's in place? I'm here to do you a service. I could be a fresh pair of eyes to see what you have in place." That cracks the door open. There are a lot of different ways to do it, but that's the one I find most effective.

DD: Let's talk about the agents reading this right now. They've never done annuities but they are interested in it. They hear that it is a large opportunity. There's a lot of money in it. What different avenues are there available for the agent to move money into an annuity?

SB: You can find annuity business in paid up cash value policies, large whole life policies, and universal life policies that are blowing up or have lost their purpose. A lot of men, particularly engineers, have giant UL policies for the benefit of their wives. Their wives have passed away, but they get used to paying on them. What's happening is that they are draining cash value. That is where you find annuities. You find them in life insurance, in the bank account, because money in the bank account is lazy.

What happens with the money that a woman gets from her husband's life insurance policy when he passes away? I moved one client's retirement funds over to an annuity contract. I helped her with a single premium on her life insurance policy. I have her on Medicare supplements. But she's got $100,000 sitting in the bank from when her father died. He left her a large amount of money and it's sitting in a bank account.

Somebody over the age of 65 that has more than 50% of their money in stocks is at risk of loss. I call it the rule of 100. The key feature on an annuity is to allow money to grow at a respectable rate, without the risk of loss. All of these people have lived through 2007-2008 when the tech bubble blew and the market dropped significantly. What most people remember is that their 401Ks disappeared. That took five years to recover from. At the age that they are at, they cannot afford to have that kind of hit to their return on their retirement investments. If they're working, they can fix it, but if they're not working then they have to wait for the market to recover. They may not have the five years to wait for the market to recover. It's going to drop their monthly income, their required mandatory distributions down rapidly. If they are in a variable annuity, they need to not be in one. If they've gone to a financial planner, they are in a variable annuity. Their money is at risk. It's not what I advise people to do at that age.

DD: Let's talk about the agent who is reading this and is interested in this opportunity. He isn't sure if this is the right thing for him. You have talked about cold calling, about there being a lot of money in annuities, and about understandable resistance. What would you say to help them determine if this opportunity is right for them?

SB: The first characteristic that I'm looking for before I start working with an agent is their field experience. Have they already been in the trial-error-trial-success mode of his or her career? I'm not going to take somebody who is absolutely new and get them started on this. It's best if they have experience in the field and if they have a good rapport with the client. Start off with the agents that have great skills, are excited, and want to move forward. What I'm offering with our new training technique is what a real annuity agent does every day. A Monday through Saturday routine. Watch what I do, pay attention to the calls, check in to see how I did on it. You see that I get the results and I do it again the next week.

If you can't do what I'm doing, you shouldn't be in the business. Once it becomes second nature, I don't need a script in front of me. I like insurance agents because they like to be their own boss. We have a lot in common. I'll call up and follow up. I remind you of your low hanging fruit. I keep you going because I know where business is. Agencies have a lot of business and they don't know it yet. We're finding an awful lot of business in the portfolios of people who go out and write final expense. It's really exciting. I'd like to see them jump in.

DD: I want to establish, for the reader, what kind of opportunity is literally just sitting out there. We've been working mutually with a guy called Jeremy for the last three months. What kind of business has he written and what kind of annuity business is he currently working on? What opportunities are out there, even amongst the same final expense leads that you're working on?

SB: Jeremy's got pixie dust and he keeps falling into it. He has a couple of people who work with him and they keep finding it. He is going after $95,000 for a whole life policy. That's a solid deal. When we first talked on the phone, I went through all of it. He described all of what he thought was his annuity business. He had this one big grapefruit that was hanging off the grapefruit tree waiting for somebody to pick it. It was a lady with a substantial amount of money that was undermanaged. A $160,000 individual retirement account. I kept asking him why he didn't pick it and he kept saying that he has been busy. He's got the right plan. He keeps what's working for him and then, in between, he plucks the low hanging fruits in his final expense business. It's been a pleasure to work with him.

How To Sell 1400 Medicare Supplements In 12 Months

Interview with Christopher Westfall of
MedicareAgentTraining.com

About Christopher Westfall

Today I have the pleasure of interviewing a longtime friend in the business, Christopher Westfall. He is a licensed insurance agent, specializing in the Medicare supplement business since 2009. He owns MedicareAgentTraining.com. He helps agents around the country succeed in the Medicare supplement business. He also operates a national call center helping seniors with their Medicare supplement needs. So far this year, Chris has qualified for five sales conventions based on production. He and his team have sold an incredible 1,369 Medicare supplement policies. There are several more days to go, so that might get over 1400, right Chris?

CW: We're going to get there!

DD: Chris, thank you so much for joining me today. Let's start from the beginning. What's your background? Where did you start in life? How did you get into insurance? What were your reasons?

CW: When I was a little kid growing up, I always wanted to help people. Superman was my hero, and I thought that the closest thing that I could be to Superman was a police officer. So at the age of five, I committed my life, long-term. I was going to be a police officer.

I started to train at 19. That's when you can start in Florida. I was the youngest one at my agency, no surprise there. I started off with a small city police department in Florida, then went to the County Sheriff's office. Three years in I was promoted to the rank of sergeant. For the next 13 years, I stayed at that rank. I looked at the next promotion level, lieutenant, and what that would make me per annum. When I was a sergeant, I could work overtime. I was making $70,000, $80,000 a year. A lieutenant's salary was capped out at $58,000 a year. I went to my superiors and asked them, "How do you expect to get quality people to move up in the ranks and accept lower pay? With a salary base of $58,000, no incentive and no overtime opportunity?"

"Well, that's just the way it is."

It was one of the lowest paid agencies in Florida. I had to do something else. I had gained my insurance license a while back, so I started doing final expense part-time. I would work two days on and two days off at the sheriff's office. I would do final expense on one of my two days off. My goal was to make $1000 a day, then quit, go home and be with the family. I hit that goal almost every day that I can remember. It really helped to supplement my income. That's how I got started doing insurance.

DD: So you came into this business like most people selling insurance. It was the last thing you ever imagined yourself doing out of Madison, correct?

CW: That's true.

DD: It's funny how we stumble into things that we have no concept of. When I was getting into insurance the last thing I ever thought about doing was life insurance. I couldn't imagine a less sexy job. Circumstance puts us in different positions. You started with final expense and today you're not

selling that. What was the transition from final expense to Medicare? Why did you make that transition?

CW: When I first got started I was all alone. I didn't know anybody else in the industry. I spent a lot of time online with insurance discussion forums. I learned from other people there. I read about their mistakes and their discoveries in the industry. I learned about the concept of a residual income. Back then, with what I was doing it felt at times like I was taking two steps forward and one step back. The concept of residual income seemed neat to me. So I started changing my focus a little, started learning about Medicare. It seemed like it was really complicated. In Florida, everything is Medicare Advantage. The Supplements that I was learning so much about, I couldn't sell those in Florida. The prices were out of whack, and the competition with Medicare Advantage was crazy.

I walked into a Mcdonald's one day and had an epiphany. I kid you not. I saw all the senior citizens sitting around. I started listening. What are they talking about? They're talking about their knee replacement or hip replacement. How great their orthopedic doctors are. Asking where their friends are. "Oh, he's sick. He's in the hospital." I noticed that everybody was talking about their health. Their doctor, their health plan. I was a life insurance agent, final expense. Nobody was talking about death and dying or what life insurance policy they had.

It so happened that at that part of the year I would see billions of dollars of advertising spent on Medicare. Everywhere. Medicare, Medicare, Medicare. I'm thinking, "Wow, that's focusing the whole senior population on one product. Medicare. Wouldn't it be neat to slip into that downstream of consciousness of Medicare? They're talking about it in McDonald's, it's all over the TV, it's on the radio, it's in the newspaper. There are full-page ads for Humana down there." I started thinking that this would be the way toward residual income. Getting into that stream, that consciousness. It's already there. In discussions, we were already there. It was something that I needed to start making a transition to.

When I left the sheriff's office, I went full time into final expense. I started making a lot more money. Then I started going from that to one day a week of focusing on Medicare. Nobody was doing it over the phone that I knew of. This was nine years ago and only one company had an electronic application. It was very difficult. It was actually sending a package through the mail to people. I sent 13 packets out and I got back 5 out of the 13. I thought, "Wow, this is amazing. I can actually sell this stuff over the phone!" Florida was not very conducive to Medicare Supplements, so I started selling in Michigan. Then I realized that I should do two days a week. I'm building monthly income, I should do three days a week. Finally, I broke free and only did Medicare.

DD: I know a lot of agents who start with one particular product, the final expense or something else. Then they see something else that they want to potentially transition to. One of the most difficult things is to walk the line for both products and be successful. You have done that. What advice would you give somebody that wants to transition from their bread-and-butter insurance lines without losing effectiveness?

CW: I have worked with about 3000 agents in the last five years, and there is a real dichotomy. I have to put this out there and be completely transparent. One type of agent is supported by their spouse, who is the breadwinner. They're out there, trying different things, more as a hobby than a profession. I can't help those guys. They don't have the level of immersion into the culture necessary to be successful. They're not going to try hard enough. If they don't understand the answer to a question, they're not going to go open an underwriting guide to get it. They get a little bit of resistance, things don't go their way, they pack it up and go home. They say, "Honey, I tried this. It didn't work."

The other type of agent burns bridges behind them. They have no more career to go back to. They've decided where to put their focus. Never mind dipping their toe in the pool. They have jumped into the deep end. They treat the business like they've invested their entire life savings. It doesn't matter what it takes, if somebody else can do it, then by God, they can do the same thing. They will figure out the answers to the things that they don't know.

Those kinds of people will succeed. No matter which focus that they go into within our industry. I know people who make a great living at long-term care. People who focus on mortgage protection term. The only thing that's unique about those people is that 100% of them burn their bridges behind them. They have nowhere else to go. You've got to make it work. I found one mentor when I got started doing it over the phone, a guy in Texas. The first FMO that I found put me in touch with him on the phone. The guy said, "Yes, it's possible. We do it all day long. Nobody else is doing it, but yes, it can be done." That's the trigger that I needed. It's all I needed to know. He didn't tell me exactly who to sell to, how to sell it, how to get the signatures over the phone. None of that detail stuff. None of the technical stuff. He simply said that the concept works. It's a proven concept and it works. With that proof of concept, I jumped all in. It's those agents who decide to do that, that make that mental decision. When they make that decision, then there's no stopping them. There's no end to the income that they can build.

DD: What you're saying is so true. There's people that don't have the fire burning underneath them to go out there and give it their all. It's because they don't have to. They have a backup plan. I work on many profiles of success, not only in life insurance or insurance in general, but success in life. Many times, the people who are successful seem to have all the odds against them. I've thought in my tougher days that if I didn't have a wife, kids, financial obligations, I'd make it. I know some people think the same thing. You've got a lot of kids. You're married. I've got a lot of kids. I'm married. They're our fire burning underneath us. If there's a will, there's a way. If you apply yourself, it's amazing the results that you can get. You're 100% right. You have to risk it all if you want the big success story. It's so true for so many successful people. Probably all of them.

CW: Very true.

DD: Your transition into Medicare took you some time. You were doing something that very few people were doing. It was the dark ages of Medicare

when we didn't have electronic applications or telephonic sales. Where there's a will, there's a way.

There are guys that love the idea of selling over the phone, but they've got a major concern. They've heard from other people that you can't sell over the phone. You have to sell face to face. What are your thoughts on the differences between selling over the phone and selling face to face? You've done both. How can you be successful either way?

CW: There's an old story about an elephant that's tethered to a rope. He can't go anywhere. They take the rope away, but he still doesn't go anywhere. He's so used to being confined within the restrictions that were placed there before. I find that that is so true in our industry. We see it every day. I'll see an older seasoned agent who's been in the business for 30, 40, 50 years. He will tell me that he's been around forever and that phone thing can't be done.

On the other hand, at 20 years old my son was selling 13 policies a week over the phone. He's never been told it can't be done. He doesn't know any different. It's the same with Millennials all over the place. One of my agents went on a company trip to Iceland with me two years ago. He was 19 years old and qualifying for a trip. How does that happen? It's because in their mind they don't have that restriction. It absolutely can be done. It's a switch in the mind. If it works, it works. Agents sometimes think that they can't do it. And they're right. Other agents see that it's being done and think, "I can do it!" They're right too.

One thing about selling over the phone that people have to realize is that it's all about scalability. It's a cookie cutter approach. I love that. Something happens on a micro level and you add scale to it and grow it to a macro level by doing the same exact thing. That's scalability. The Bible says, "One shall chase a thousand, and two put ten thousand to flight." It's growing exponentially.

That's what I've found here in my office. Selling over the phone, I could see ten people in an hour and a half or two hours. I could have a conversation with them to see if it's going to go anywhere. To prospect them and see if there's any qualification there to move forward. Doing the same thing in the field, I can reach three clients in a day. Five. Eight if I push it for an all-day event. I'm talking about an hour and a half here of getting through the "yes, no, yes, no, yes, no."

Mike Brooks has a wonderful training called the top 20%. He studied how the top 20% of phone salespeople from all different industries separate themselves from the other 80%. The key difference is sorting early. Eliminate, as quick as you can, those people who you're not going to move forward with. Don't be nice and have a conversation. They will talk to you all day and never stop. You have to separate the wheat from the chaff. Take the best that you can and tell everybody else, "I'm sorry. You're in a good position. Stay where you're at."

You can do that kind of scalability over the phone so much more than you can do it face to face. You don't have windshield time; driving to see people. To agents who say, "Oh no, people won't buy over the phone," take it from me, they buy over the phone all day long. Imagine that you can talk to 10 times as many people over the phone, have a conversation with them and weed them out. Let's say that you're 50% as effective. You're only going to close half of what you would have closed if you were face to face. But, you can talk to 10 times as many people. It's that margin of scalability that gives a 50% minimum boost on my income. In my office, I've got five other agents all talking on the phone at the same time to people. They're bringing in more and more quality people. There are so many people out there, so many policies. They start referring. Imagine that on a mass scale. All your existing clients are happy with your emails, your cards in the mail. Based on that, they start referring people. It starts to grow like a mushroom cloud.

You might only be 20% as efficient selling over the phone. Still, you have made a huge improvement on what you can do relying on your tires, the oil in your car and the gas in your tank. I drive a Tesla now, I don't have to pay for gas, but for those who drive gas cars, you don't have to worry about that. You're sitting there and you're 10 times more productive. I like doing it in spurts. I'm not prospecting, I have other people do that. I sit there, do a whole bunch of qualifying. Qualify, qualify, qualify, get up, go to lunch, have a good time hanging out. I still accomplish more in that day than an agent who gets up, drives an hour or two to their work area and then starts knocking on doors. The effectiveness and the scalability is what's all about.

DD: *Let's expand on the scalability from the perspective of a newer agent that wants to jump into Medicare sales. What activities that they're doing can be scaled or outsourced in order for them to spend more time with qualified prospects?*

CW: When I first got started, I worked with somebody in the Philippines. I learned that you can telemarket using $3 an hour labor instead of $25 like I was used to at the sheriff's office. $3 labor with me on the phone all the time. Then I started reading books such as "The Four Hour Work Week" by Tim Ferriss. Books about people who have scaled up their business so much by outsourcing. I went to a website, found a woman named Beverly. She was with me for over three years. I had to go through five other people that didn't work out before I found her. Every day she got better and better. Every day she would go out and prospect with my simple script. She would ask if people would like to save money on their Medicare supplement plan. She would ask if they had been in the hospital in the last year. It was very basic at the time. I would get a list every day of people who were interested in talking to me.

Then I transitioned her into saying, "If you're interested, I'm going to put you on the phone with Mr. Westfall." She would build me up, edify me before I got on the phone. That was key. She would then give them a website. They would spend some time on my website. They would see me, hear me, find out that they like and trust me before we even got on the phone. My level of credibility when I finally got on the phone was way up there. That was a big difference. I no longer had to prospect and that, I find with agents, is 90% of the stress of doing the Medicare business. The prospecting and the constant rejection.

The good thing is that there are people on the other side of the world who would kill to do that for $3 an hour. They are loyal and they will show up every day. They speak 90% grade English. Good enough to be effective at helping you scale your business. My son is 22, He's got seven telemarketers on the other side of the world constantly feeding him new leads every day. He's talking to the cream of the crop only. He's found that he's cranking out applications all the time because he's no longer doing the $3 an hour work. Work is valued at the lowest price that somebody is willing to do it for. If you are making $100,000 a year, but you're doing $3 hour labor, you're wasting time! Somebody else is willing to do that. Even if they can't do it at 50% of your effectiveness. Let them to do it and scale them up at $3 an hour so that you can do the bigger things. Qualify people and get in the applications. In my case, I found another licensed insurance agent and put him in the qualifying seat. I went from cold calling to having a qualifier who only set appointments for me to do the applications. That's when everything started rocketing up.

DD: Chris, you have a program in which you help agents in the Medicare business. I do exactly what you're talking about, finding reps overseas for qualifications. Can you talk a little bit about that for anybody who's interested in leveraging the same?

CW: I started telling that story a couple of years ago. You don't have a big social media presence, or buy online leads and go to the Internet conferences all year. How could you best position yourself? I study that stuff. They have a limited budget to get their business started. I tell them that they should start like I did, with a telemarketer.

Now we have a business called TrainedTelemarketers.com. That business consists of a team of people both in the US and in the Philippines. They recruit, train and get people set up on the predictive dialers. Those people are then ready to go. They're turnkey and they just go at it. We've sold 350 telemarketers through that service in the last year. A lot of those agents go on to have contracts with me, a lot don't. But what I've seen in my agency is a massive increase in its production. It reminds me of that old saying, "A rising tide raises all ships."

I think we're number seven as an agency in the United States for Cigna production this year. That's solely because the agents have people to prospect. They've got somewhere to go to get that off their plate. I'm not trying to pitch trained telemarketers. I'm saying that we saw a need, so we created that service. Everybody's spending so much time trying to find the great client. We figured that we should make an entity, put a team together that does nothing but that. Then the agent can go back to selling and doing what they do best.

DD: Thank you for explaining that. I've had a couple of agents that work with me that have done business with TrainedTelemarketers.com. They love it and they've had great success with it. There's a lot of guys that would benefit from that. I wanted to make sure that we mentioned it.

You use a lot of social media. it's something that I use as well, especially in my recruiting business. It works fantastically well. How important is social media as a source of prospecting for your Medicare supplement business? How would you suggest agents incorporate social media into their business models to become more successful?

CW: I'm in a unique position. I decided to go all in with social media when I moved to South Carolina and left my marketing people behind. I started to put out content on YouTube and Facebook, then synthesize that content and spread it out all over the Internet. Every year we've been lucky to go on a bunch of company trips. We went to Berlin last year, Iceland and Rome, all these far away places. It's been beautiful. We meet agents there, the top producers from all these companies, they always get together. About the third night of the trip, the discussion comes up:

"Well, how do you get business?"

"This is how you get business."

Discussion follows. Young guys that run call centers will always have a debate about their cost of client acquisition. They discuss how many months out it will be on the residual income train before they're profitable on what they spent to acquire that customer.

I'll sit there and listen quietly because my cost of acquisition is zero. It doesn't cost a thing to get the 1300 policies that we've got so far this year. They don't understand that. We are getting into an age where the giant corporations are trying to encroach upon anything that is direct to consumer. We're seeing Amazon now coming into the pharmacy space. It's going to totally disrupt that space. It's been direct to the consumer before, by everybody else who's tried it. The likes of Amazon and Walmart have started pushing Medicare Supplements. It's the same scenario because they are commoditized. They have started pushing those products direct to consumer with a billion dollar budget. What can the independent agent do?

I would argue that the only way to remain relevant as an independent agent is to start working on your brand. You have to be found. If you or your marketing team start the conversation with somebody, they want to know who you are. When they Google search you - and they will Google search you - what are they going to find? You can control 100% of what they find online. You can control the reviews. You can control where you're found online, what they see about you, your message that you get out there.

I've found that when people call in, they don't want to know who I am. They don't want to know what I have. They want to know what they should do. They will say, "Hey, I'm calling in because I saw Chris' video on this topic. What plan should I go with? Here's my zip code, tell me." Then they sign up. It goes back to that. People buy from who they know, like and trust. That's the weird thing about working online. You put your message, your branding, out there all the time. They will already know you when they call in. They feel like they've known you forever.

I have a great story to tell. I've lived in South Carolina now for years. This week, the second client that we ever got here came into my office and I saw them in person. The second one. I've got his photograph around here somewhere. I took a picture of it because it's so unusual for someone to come in like that. He came in and shook my hand. He happened to be passing through town going to a wedding. He wanted to see me and shake my hand for all the help that our staff gave him, saving him money on his Medicare plan. The thing is that when he walked in he said, "I feel like I'm meeting a celebrity!"

It's weird, but it happens all the time. We get together with agent training events. We did two live events where agents came from around the country this past year. When they come here they say things like, "Wow, you're taller than I imagined, but I feel like I know you because I watch all this stuff that you put out on video."

Even on a small level, even if you don't want to become a YouTube star, every agent should control the conversation. When somebody searches you, what are they going to find? You need to build that picture as a brand or else be lost in the sea of commodity, full of every other insurance agent. This weekend my big project is working on reviewing websites that my agents have. They've asked me to review their websites to see how they can improve. The biggest thing that I'm finding is that their websites are stuffy or boring. Corporate looking. Sterile. There's no kind of personality to them. Nothing jumps out and says, "Hi, I'm a person. Let me solve your needs." That's what agents have to do if they're going to remain relevant in a world of commoditization. Amazon and Walmart, all these companies are looking to come in. What's going to separate you from everybody else?

First, you have to grab their attention. You can do that through a myriad of ways, but once you have it, you have to keep it. They have to know you as a person. You can't hide behind a 16 point font, black text on white background. On a website, they've got to be drawn into you. You have to build a connection with them. Otherwise, you're just like everybody else out there trying to sell something.

DD: I agree with you. Look at the business world as it stands. Anywhere where there is a middleman, he's being eliminated. Amazon is at the forefront of it. So many traditional businesses are shuttering up. They've been long-term successful, but now everything's changed.

I've always told agents that we're a necessary evil. Companies are always looking for ways to eliminate any costs. We're a cost component to doing the business by adding value in different ways. We have to. But it will affect us in some way. As time goes on, postage prices are going up, it will be more expensive. We are competing constantly in those markets to make a living.

It's very sensible to take time to invest in yourself and improve upon those things as you do.

We hear now about robots doing human work. The advent of automation and technological advancements such as these creates a whole radical change in how business is being done. Where do you see the insurance business, specifically the Medicare supplement area, in the next 10 to 20 years? What will agents have to do to continue high levels of production?

CW: The good thing is that there will always be a need for the insurance agent. Look at what the government is spending. The majority of the budget is on what they call entitlements. My clients get mad when they hear the word entitlement. "I'm not entitled," they say, "I earn that Medicare benefit!" And they're right. The government is spending all this money on the entitlement part of the budget; Social Security, Medicare, and Medicaid. They're going to have to pay that back. Either pay it back or go bankrupt and shut down. That's not going to happen. In the next couple of years, we're going to see (if it's still Republican) Congress trying to find some way to cut back Social Security for the younger people like us. We're never going to get it. Medicare benefits will also be cut back to some extent, or transitioned more to the private partnership. Private companies running Medicare. All of those things are going to require an agent to step in with a solution.

Going back to focusing on Medicare Supplements versus Medicare Advantage. At the Medicare convention last year, some girl who is a representative of an FMO got really angry at me. We're having one of those evening discussions in the bar about Medicare. "What do you mean, you don't go after Medicare Advantage," she said. "You're rich and you're discriminating against the people who are poor!"

DD: It's discrimination! It would, of course, come to that!

CW: There are so many agents who are used to only doing Medicare Advantage. It usually costs nothing. They just need a signature in there. Done. The idea of getting somebody to pay a premium for an insurance policy is foreign to many agents. I don't understand it. There are many seniors who have actually done this thing called saving money for retirement. People who have a pension from a good incorporation, all that stuff. They want more than the government is willing to allow. Especially when that government benefit starts chipping down, going away. The loss of their benefits has made a hole. What they want and expect from their old corporate lives to fill that hole and what the government is willing to give are going to get further and further apart.

That's where the agent will always have an advantage by coming in with a supplemental benefit. It might be a cancer policy, a life policy that they're not going to get, with the burial from the government. The Medicare supplement bridges that gap between what's available and what they expect. They've got the money to pay for it. It's said that the biggest transfer of wealth is happening in this generation, from the baby boomers to the younger generation. These people have money. Don't be fooled into thinking that they're all broke, they're all destitute. They're not. And those people who have money will always pay for the better benefits. There's always going to be a position for agents to come in there and provide that need for them. Especially those with the money. They value a consultation service and they will pay for it. In many ways that's a great thing. Having insurance agents come in and help them with their insurance is something that the majority still want. It's not like other sales positions. We're not used cars salesman yet! These people find out that it doesn't cost a dime more to have my personalized individual health plan than if you went straight to the carrier. "Let me help you for free," I say. "My advice is free. I get paid by the company."

When they hear that, they say, "Oh, why wouldn't I work with you? I don't want to call a call center, a big corporation. I'd love to have your health plan." It definitely works.

DD: What do you think is the number one reason that agents fail in the insurance business? It's going to go back to a lot of what we said in the beginning. There's so much opportunity here. Why do 90% plus fail within the first year?

CW: Let me put it this way. Opening a Mcdonald's franchise that you have saved up your whole life for. Mortgaging your house. Borrowing from your in-laws, every dime that you can muster from everybody around you. Being motivated to go in and make this work. Being at your Mcdonald's, working from day to night, hiring the team, working with the team. Inspiring the team to make sure that everything in the restaurant is set up correctly. Knowing full well that you're not going to make a dime on your investment, no ROI whatsoever, for the first five years.

That kind of commitment is the mindset that's needed to work in this industry and make it a 100% success. The problem with the industry is there's such a low barrier to entry. For $200 and 40 hours of sitting in a classroom with a pie in the sky dream, you can get your license. An agent thinks that they're going to be a millionaire based on the fact that they've got that license. I get voicemails every week from agents who say, "I'm a licensed agent. I'm calling you because I'm going to talk to you about my business. I'm a licensed agent." Well, that license and $1.50 might get you a crappy cup of coffee at Mcdonald's. It's not worth a doggone thing, that license.

If they treated it as if they spent eight or twelve years of medical school to get it, that is the value of what it holds. The inherent value of that license is what you do with it. They don't appreciate or value enough what that license could do for them. Could they make over a million dollars a year in residual income? Have a staff of people that are super happy because they do trips together all the time? Yes, they could. What would it take to do that? That little license?

It's the mindset of "Wow, how far can we go? How big can we scale this up?" I know call center owners in their twenties in Florida whose centers are doing 400 policies a week. They see the vision, they want to run with it, they're willing to work day and night for it. They're not accepting any excuses. They've caught the vision and they know that it works.

There are agents who do not have the expectation that if they don't get off their butt and do something with it, they're going to be on the street next week. They have no vision, no drive, no motivation. The insurance license is completely useless to them. It's a waste of time. They need to go get a job where somebody hits them on the ass every day and says, "You need to clock in. Don't clock in late." We all know people like that. They're better off in an hourly job.

But there are people who are driven by incentive, by the goal of doing something much better than any employer could ever offer them. It takes that kind of mindset. The most important thing is working on mindset. Working on training your brain as to what's available out there, what's possible to do. Working on you yourself. It's not the technical thing of "What product can I sell today or where? Where's the best market? What's the secret script? There's gotta be a secret script behind it!" All that stuff is crap and it doesn't matter.

Jim Rome says, "What you lack in skill, you can make up in numbers." It's so true in this business. If you prospect 10 times more than the guy who barely gets out of bed, but he's good on the phone, then you're going to win. You're going to beat him every time. You can do that if you're doing a scalable business where you can prospect 10 times more people.

It all comes down to motivation, mindset and making that decision that you've got the best opportunity available out there. "It only cost me $200 to get here. But look what I can do. I know that I can make a million dollars a year if I work at it long and hard enough to get good people to come in and work with me."

Many people are afraid of hiring people. They think that they can't afford that. I thought the same thing when I hired my first assistant. how could I afford that? Then I started to double my business based on his production. I got another person in here to help me. Now I'm tripling my business. Even if my margin is half as much, I've got a team of five people. Oh my gosh, we're doing so much more business. Look at the compounding effect of residual income. We could sell 1300 policies this year, each one worth $1,500. We did the same thing last year. Our monthly income continues to go up based on that.

It's catching the dream, catching the vision, putting it into action and not quitting. Even when you have the little obstacles that are inherent in any business. You know you're going to have obstacles. My training help, or anybody else's that's out there, can't cover every single situation and nuance, every weird thing that can happen. It's what you do on those margins, when you're on your own. You have to either call the carrier and get help, ask another agent, look on an online form or figure it out yourself. What do you do? You could quit, saying that it's too complicated, you're out of this business. Or you could press on. Become a business owner. Act like an entrepreneur. That's the difference between a business person versus an employee. If they've got the business owner mindset, they treat it like they've invested a lot into it. You can't lose with a system that works.

DD: Well said. I'd like to add a personal thought here. In a way, all of us should be thankful that this business is tough and that people do fail. If it was easy, everybody would be doing it. We'd be paid a clerk's wage. There's a reason why we face the difficulties that every single person who's made it has to face. I always tell people, "Look, if you haven't seriously thought about quitting this job at one point, you haven't been in the business long enough." There are very few people that go through this unscathed. That's part of the trial by fire process that every agent must go through in order to achieve high levels of success. It's the way it is. I've learned to embrace that instead of complaining. It's much better than working for the Man.

Chris, remind everybody. Where can we find you? Where can we learn more about you? Where can we talk to you about Medicare or learn about your training?

CW: Let me preface this by saying it was not my idea to help other agents. When I first got started, when I was doing this stuff over the phone, I came up with this online signature method. Back in the day, we used a pdf application for Medicare Supplements. That's all we had. We could do a screen share with a pen tool from Adobe Acrobat. The customer could write their signature using the mouse in their home. When I came up with that process, a big FMO by the name of Amerilife started spreading the word. People started wanting to sell over the phone. I started getting hundreds of calls from agents saying, "How are you doing that? What are you doing?" So I put together a website to show what I was doing.

Six months or a year later I realize there are 600 people that are members of this website. I'm wondering if I should charge money so that I could spend more time on it and be compensated for helping people for free. So I started a membership site and it's called MedicareAgentTraining.com. On that website, I chronicle what we're finding that works, what's happening with the carriers, what the new opportunities are. Stuff like that. It's very basic, but it's helped a lot of people. So far, 2800 people have come back and said this is positive.

It helped me get ramped up. Now I'm on my own, doing my own thing. There's not a lot of training out there for actual prospecting, actual closing, actually doing a Medicare conversation over the phone and then figuring out how to grow and scale your business. I figured I'd fill something in the niche there. That's what that is.

DD: *Perfect. Chris, thank you so much for joining me today.*

How To Close 43% Of Your Final Expense Leads

Interview with John Dugger

About John Dugger

I am sitting down with Mr. John Dugger, one of the principal people that brought me into this business. I want to give you a little bit of introduction first because you're going to be in for a nice treat; a deep dive into how an expert final expense agent operates.

John has written in excess of $2,250,000 in final expense business since he started. Before getting into final expense sales, he wrote approximately a million dollars in term insurance and almost a thousand Medicare Advantage plans. Last year, at the end of his 2017 production, he had written $235,000 in final expense on 320 applications and probably another $50,000 selling other insurance other plans like Medicare Supplements.

He is closing approximately 43% of his final expense leads. For every lead that he buys, he's writing about $318 in premium. To put this into perspective, a good agent will write $150 of premium per lead.

DD: Did I get those numbers right there, John?

JD: Yeah, pretty close.

DD: Let's talk about some actual play-by-play techniques and strategies that you use to sell final expense face to face.

JD: Well, I get 15 leads a week still. I did go to 10 a little over a year and a half ago. I get a lot of referrals, so I don't need 15 a week to get my goal. I write way over my goal because I get more leads than I need. My goal from the beginning has always been $100,000 a year, after lead costs. That's not including renewals. I'm talking $100,000 of newly written business in a year.

That's where I'm at now. I write much more than I need because I've got more leads than I can get to. My leads come in every Thursday. I call on Monday to set appointments for Tuesday, and likewise on Wednesday for Thursday. That's my typical schedule. Two days in the field. There are always exceptions to everything. Today I'm delivering policies that are not in the area that I'm working tomorrow. I've already set my appointments for tomorrow, so I'll know where I'm going to be. If I have time between appointments, I'll call some people, or if I have some that don't have numbers, I'll door knock those.

My normal week is to set six appointments for each field day.

DD: So, six appointments a day is your goal?

JD: Six in a day is plenty for me. I'll go to six tomorrow, then my plan is also to set six appointments for Thursday. But that depends on how tomorrow goes. It took Travis Tubbs (one of my mentors) years and years to get me to do this. If I go out tomorrow and write $4,000, I might not make appointments Thursday. I might not sit around the house either, you know, there are bills to be paid. But I won't care if I make any. I might make two or three for that day. It just depends. That is my normal schedule. I won't schedule more than one day out. If I'm calling for tomorrow, I'm only setting appointments for tomorrow.

I learned from an agent at National Agents Alliance to set appointments on Monday for Tuesday and Wednesday for Thursday appointment setting. He said, "You have to learn to tell people who want appointments for any other day than tomorrow, 'No.' No, I'm not going to be there Thursday, I'm going to be there tomorrow." I wasn't really sure, but he said, "You'll just have to do that."

"Well, what if that makes them mad?" I asked.

"Well, who cares?"

That was a hard lesson for me, that was very tough for me. I came back from that meeting and I did that. I was amazed that it worked. You learn over time. There are reasons that people can't meet with you the next day, which are not just excuses. It takes a long time for you to figure out which is which. I can tell now, when I'm talking and they tell me their excuse why they can't meet me. I'll talk to them a little bit more. One of the guys I talked to this morning, his excuse was that he was going to the doctor tomorrow. So I asked, "When's your appointment?"

"10:00 am."

"You'll be back by 1:00 pm, right?"

"Yes."

"Ok then, I'll see you then and there."

Then he said, "Look, I'm going to Nashville." So that's a guy I'm going to call back. He's going to be gone all day if he's going to Nashville. If he was going to the doctor five miles down the road, I would not have bought that excuse, but you learn over time which is which.

Recently I sat down and made my appointments and I scheduled my six appointments for the next day in 15 minutes. Everybody said, "OK, see you tomorrow!" That makes me more nervous than anything.

DD: *Almost too easy. What's the catch?*

JD: There are no-shows. But that's my normal schedule, that's how I like to work. Being in the field two days a week and making new appointments. Then doing the service work that I can't get to during my days of appointments on

Monday and Wednesday afternoons. Then I scrub the apps and do administration work on Friday.

DD: *You seem to have a higher than average appointment setting rate.*

JD: I get challenged a lot about getting 10-12 appointments a week on 15 leads. Well, they're probably right. If you don't have any leads and you get 15, or if you send me 15 leads right now that have never worked before, you probably won't have 10-12 appointments scheduled next week.

Now, I get a lot of referrals that supplement my leads. I didn't get a whole lot of referrals for the first two years. I'm in my 15th year now. I got a referral just last week that I went and wrote. I wrote this couple in 2011, seven years ago, and she referred her brother to me. I was looking at this couple. He passed away, so it was just her now, but they had also referred me to her other brother back then. I wrote him and two friends. So, I already have five policies written in that house. And now, after seven years, I'm getting a sixth one. He called me Friday to tell me that his ex-wife and daughter are going to call me this week. They want insurance too. If they call me, it would be eight policies written in that house. They were a referral. I had forgotten that when I was there last week, but he reminded me.

"You know, Judith was the one who sent us to you. Did you know that she passed away?"

"Yes," I said, "I did know that she passed."

I had forgotten that she sent me. She was a direct mail lead, $15 a month. She started with $15 a month. None of them were big. The one I wrote last week started at $5 a month. All the others were for $25, $30. None of them were big, but we're talking six applications right now and he's telling me two more. So who knows?

DD: *What do you do when you get into the presentation? Are you the kind of agent that focuses on building rapport and then goes into a cross-selling routine? How do you start your presentation? Can you walk us through from the start to the finish?*

JD: Well, I tell everybody, the first step in the sales process is setting your own appointments. That's how I treat it. I've got a leg up when I go in. I have already spoken to these homes. I don't do any qualifying on the phone, even when they try to talk about it. Some people do. I will discuss that the next day. When I get there, I introduce myself and I go back over the lead card. Then I explain why I'm there, why I called them, and we go over the lead card together. We find one of three reasons why people mail this card. The number one reason is that they don't have anything in place to take care of their final expense burial. The number two reason is that they have all that taken care of, they've got something in place now, but don't think it's enough. More and more often people want to see if they are paying too much for what they have. The third reason is that they want to leave some money to their family, their church, leave a legacy of some sort.

It's not a good sign when you have to ask them, "Which one of those reasons is yours?" Usually, if you have to ask that, it's because they weren't listening to you the first time. Then you've got a problem because you won't get an acknowledgment. Then you've got to recheck yourself. You got to tell yourself, "Ok, they weren't listening to me first time. Now we've got to start over, to find out why they mailed out that card." If they can't give me a reason at all, I leave. I do not present to uninterested people. If you cannot give me a reason why you mailed out that card, have a nice day.

DD: That's so hard for agents to do, isn't it John?

JD: Well, I wouldn't tell any new agent to do that. I'm going to know whether they are buying or not, but a new agent might miss that. Even if they're not buying, I'd go ahead and present, because if anything, you get to practice your presentation.

I don't talk people into buying anything. I'm not about that. I have to do my presentation the way I do it. I'm not good at overcoming objections. I don't talk people into appointments. If you don't want to see me, I'm ok with that. I'd rather you tell me you don't want to see me than set an appointment and not show up. I'm not talking you in to an appointment, I'm not begging to see you.

I want people to buy what they want. People don't buy what they need. They buy what they want and what they can afford, of course. I might need a new car as well, but I'm not going to buy if I can't afford it.

Everybody is bad at putting their own value on things. I do it with door knocking. You have to fight that. I don't like door knocking because I don't want to be door knocked. I don't want someone showing up at my house unsolicited trying to tell me something. It irritates me when someone does that. I don't want to do to people what I don't want done to me. Most of our people probably don't mind the door knocking. But it doesn't matter. It matters to me more. That just doesn't work for me.

Some agents even call people by their first names. I understand why they do that, but it doesn't work for me. I always call people Mr. and Mrs. until they tell me different. People will do that; "Mr. Jones is my Dad's name. You can call me Jim." But, if they don't say that, they'll be Mr. and Mrs. as long as I know them.

Truly the presentation doesn't matter if you find people's 'why', meaning the reason that they need insurance. I'm not comfortable with the money purchase thing, so I don't do that.

DD: *You mean selling the premium, as Tim Winders does?*

JD: Yes, exactly. I don't like that. When I go buy a car, I go by my own purchase price. Every car salesman is trying to sell you on monthly payments. I'll get you into this for $350 a month. It might be for 12 years! Once you get that money commitment, there's the hope. It's not as much about the presentation as it is about finding their 'why'. No why, no buy!

DD: *That's right!*

JD: You've got a lot of people saying Tim Winders lines. Tim was a great agent, with a great presentation. If I wasn't in this business, I would probably choose Tim as my agent. He inspires that trust when you talk to him. People are saying Travis Tubbs lines, but they are not writing business on Travis Tubbs lines. You have Jose Arteaga, who has done $330,000 last year on 20 leads a week, setting his own appointments. He got the same training as so many others did. You have Nick Frumkin. Some people are just born for this. They are great at this. Guys like Travis Tubbs, Nick Frumkin, Jose Arteaga, and others. They really have to work at it, spend time learning this stuff. If you will do that, then this business is so rewarding, setting your own schedule and making it happen. If you apply what they teach you, you can do great. Just do what I did when I went with NAA. I just learned that system and applied it word for word. There were things in that system that I didn't like. I hated saying those things, but I said them because I didn't know how to sell insurance.

DD: That is so true. I tell agents all the time, "You have to be a good soldier and follow orders. You have to earn the right to question it. If you ever get to that point, it will have only been through trial and tribulation. There's a reason you're told what to say. You're told because it works and has probably worked for a lot of other people. Simplify your life and just do what you're told."

JD: The best lessons have to be learned. Just like one leggers. I was told not to do one leggers. But I thought mine were different, "I can do one leggers. I don't care what other people are saying." Today, I would tell you not to do one leggers.

If we're talking about the market, it's about the people. It's not about the product. You get a lot of advice in this business from people who don't sell final expense. They might sell other types of life insurance, but not final expense. Those agents are not dealing with what we're dealing with. They do not understand the market of the people and it's about that market. Some of the best agents I know out there don't know the first thing about what a UL is or the difference between a UL and a GUL. When we say that the UL is imploding, they don't know what in the world we're talking about. But those agents are writing tons of business. They're just doing what they are taught.

Understand the people. Read and react. I've had that conversation many times with Nick. What is our people's interest, what is their 'wow', what's important to them. What's important to people who are world class procrastinators is different from what's important to the average person. I'm not saying that's wrong. It's different. If you think it's wrong, that will come across when you are in people's homes. You're not going to make it in this business. Lots of people can't stand to work what we do, and that's fine. I understand that.

Understand what's going on in their home. Why did they send this card in? Why do they have you in their house? They all have a 'why'. They might forget it and not ever meet with you. But they know that the card that they sent in is about insurance. They do. It took me forever to realize that. They all know. They've been getting these cards for years. They've sent other cards in over the past 6 to 12 months. They've met with other agents. In a thousand people, you may find one for whom it is the first card they ever mailed. You are the first guy they ever talked to. That could happen, but as you know, you can't build your business on the exceptions. Once you have a 'why' and you have a myriad of companies to write, you are going to leave the house with an application. The only exception to that being if they don't have any money.

You have to get their walls down. You know when the walls come down, you see that when you're talking to them. If you proceed with walls up, you're not going to sell to that person even if you've got what they want. You have to be a student of this business. Understand what they're looking for. Learn to know if they're listening to you when you talk. I've started presentations in homes where I could tell they're not listening to me and that they are not buying. You can tell that they don't like you and you are not going to sell that person anything. You've got to understand that and cut your time in there short. You can't spend your time with that person.

And no-shows. You just can't get upset about no-shows. Travis calls them agent killers. Thank God for them. If not for them, they thin the herd.

DD: With your experience in this business, where do you think final expense is going to be in 10-20 years? Do you think we're going to be doing the exact same thing that we're doing right now? Do you see the lead generation process changing? Face to face falling out of favor? What's your overall opinion?

JD: It's going to change. Change is inevitable. But it will be the last market to change and they will never change completely over. I used to say that the next card I have that has an email or sends a text will be my first. Now I say that the next one I have might be my fifth or sixth. The fundamentals will not change. That's what people outside looking in don't get and will never get. The folks in final expense are world class procrastinators. They haven't been good with their money. They didn't get to be 65 or 75 years old and not have their final expenses taken care of because they've been proactive and good with their money. Most of them have a thing about 'the man'. They feel disenfranchised. I don't think anyone who doesn't sell final expense will ever understand what I'm saying, even if I talk to them all day about it.

David, you know this because you are someone who recruits and trains: The people who can do this, can do this. They pretty much hit the ground running because they just get it. They get better as time goes along, but they can either do this or they can't. That is my theory. You can tell me if I'm wrong on that. That's what I've seen over the years. In my 15 years in insurance, 10 in final expanse, I have never yet seen an agent that struggled and struggled for months in final expense and then the light came on and they became good at this.

DD: I always tell agents that there are three categories that they could fit in. I call it the 60-30-10 rule.

There's 10% that are just studs. You know, they just get out there and they're exactly like you've described.

Then there is 60% of them that don't. They have endless excuses. Fill in the blanks. They're just not going to be successful.

Then there's a middle 30% where I see agents that have the capability to be at the top. They could be in the 10%, but there's something stopping them. It's usually a personal issue. It's not a leads issue. Sometimes it is, but very rarely. I'd say that 80% of the time, it's a work ethic problem. It is an avoidance behavior problem with selling. I can think of several agents right off the top of my head that could have the stuff. The question becomes, will

they ever have the stuff? I don't think it's something I could solve. I can just show them the way. They have to decide to take that path.

I think you're either going to instinctively understand this market or not. I tell agents now that one of the biggest objections is, "I have to put all this money into this business. What if it doesn't work?"

So I'll tell him, "Look, if you give this a solid month, you go out there and you see all these people, I'm not going to say you're going to make a huge amount of money, but you should break even, at least, if not do better than that. You'll know. If you do this month, you'll know if this is for you."

JD: I am 100% convinced that you cannot learn this business from someone who does not know how to do this. I'm not saying that people who have never qualified for trips are not good, but I can tell you that any agent just qualified for these companies' trips is the real deal. They don't pass those trips out.

Like I said earlier, new agents just don't know the right questions to ask the person that's training them. I didn't either. When a person is teaching you, you'll hear him talk about referrals. He is teaching you the system; "I have a system on getting referrals."

"How'd that work out for you when you were doing it," you ask. "How is that working out for you?"

You're getting all the referrals. You will find the person training you never got referrals. "How come you didn't produce when you were in the field," you ask. "How come you didn't produce if you were so good at this?" You just can't let that person who can't do this train you.

Now, if you want to be in their position, if you want to be recruiting agents and be a marketer, let the person training you tell you what they're doing. But if your goal is to learn to get out and sell, you have to learn from a person who has been there. A person like the guys that I mentioned earlier. People that I got with, who actually do this. If you can be with Tim Winders and let him train you, you can't go wrong there. If you want to succeed in this business, you learn from someone who is where you want to be. Don't learn from a guy riding the bench when you can learn from a star. That would be my advice to any new agent.

Top Strategies to Sell Life Insurance Online

Interview with Jeff Root of Digital IBGA

About Jeff Root

Jeff helps life insurance agents through his business online and over the phone. He is the author of the 'The Digital Life Insurance Agent'. He also does a podcast called 'The Modern Life Insurance Selling Podcast'. His agency generates over 12,000 leads monthly for his agents through websites that he has developed over at Selltermlife.com. Today we are going to be talking about selling life insurance in the digital age.

DD: Thank you very much for joining me today, Jeff.

JR: Absolutely. Glad to be here, Dave.

DD: Would you tell us a little bit about yourself and how you got started in the life insurance business?

JR: I was supposed to be an attorney. My parents were attorneys. I was straight out of college and my dad sat me at one of his meetings with his financial advisor. He wanted to help me to get a grasp of money and investing. He had his life insurance, his long-term care, his disability, his health insurance, everything with him. It piqued my interest in this meeting. His financial advisor was with Northwestern Mutual. He invited me to his office to sit with him for a day and I loved it. He had the autonomy of going to lunch whenever he wanted to, he could put on TV in the background. It rubbed me the right way, so I got started with Northwestern Mutual in 2006. My entire growth in this business is due to mentors and that started with him getting me into this business. Then a guy at Northwestern Mutual took me under his wing and showed me the ropes. I was there for a year, but I wouldn't have lasted the full year if it wasn't for that one guy.

Along the way, I have always felt that I can meet new people and mentor them. That's where I am right now. At the end of the year at Northwestern Mutual, I bought leads because I ran out of my natural market. I was some fresh face, pimply kid trying to sell life insurance investments to people double my age and it just wasn't working. I sold a few of those leads over the phone, but they didn't want to meet with me. I started losing sales to other life insurance companies. I decided, "I can be independent!"

Everything launched from there. In 2009 I bought my first URL, rootfin.com, and it's been pumping out daily leads since 2010. I have never looked back from there. I have honed my skills in internet marketing and selling over the phone. I also gained some experience in a call center. To me, that was a mentorship process; learning how to sell in bulk over the phone, making three, four, five, six sales a day. I was getting that experience and from there at the same time building websites to generate leads. I didn't need them anymore for leads. I have snowballed in the last five years, building what I have and teaching other agents how to do the same. Of course, agents are resourceful. They search things. Agents started to ask me, "Hey, how did you get to the top of Google? Is this working? This actually works? How do you do that?" So I started the blog 'Sell Term Life', which grew into the podcast because I don't like blogging. I'd rather talk. It took off from there. I wrote the book because I can't have conversations long enough with everybody to spill everything out.

DD: So you got into the business via what we could call the traditional route. You got into the captive environment. Northwestern Mutual was more

like a New York lifestyle; suit and tie, stodgy, professional. Now you're at the point where you're running your business out of your home or your own office. You're selling over the internet, sight unseen, to people across the nation. That is quite the transformation. You wrote 'The Digital Life Insurance Agent' because there's a lot to know about selling over the phone and utilizing the web to develop a presence to generate leads. Why do you think it's necessary for all agents to develop some sort of web presence in the current year of 2018?

JR: You're building a digital asset. That's so important right now. It's not just for lead generating. Everybody thinks that you need the website to generate leads. It's also for trust, pre-sale and post-sale, and it's easy to do. If one of your clients wants to refer you, it is easy to write down your URL. It's easy to remember. It's easier to recall than your phone number. Your websites have everything on there. Everything about you and what you do. Your phone number, how to contact you. Even information that could answer questions that they may have for you already. If somebody wants to refer you, they can refer people to your website to check you out. They can read the 'About' page, learn about you and your family and what you like to do. They can see your expertise on your blog or whatever it is. It's a trust builder, it always has been.

When I speak with agents who don't have a website, I'm communicating with them through a Gmail or a Hotmail account. People will tell you that it looks unprofessional. For me, I don't know anything about that person. When I get an email from an agent and it's from his website I think, "Oh cool, I get to read up about this guy before I communicate with him." It's not simply for generating leads. It builds trust with your clients. They are searching you. You need to get your name on your website. Even if they can't remember your website address, they're going to search your name. It's easy to rank for your name in Google. So if you have a website, put an 'About' page and a couple of pages of content in. You're going to rank for your name within a month or two, for that reason alone. People can find you, learn about you, see that you are legit, see your license numbers.

It's not only for clients either, it's for business in general. I communicate with agents, you communicate with agents. To see their email address, communicate with carriers, have a central hub for everything. It brings everything together. It humanizes you without the effort of having to get on the phone or have a face-to-face meeting. For me it's essential. It's so easy and it's so cheap.

DD: *My entire website is based on the principles that you have taught me through your programs. I agree with what you're saying here. The great thing about websites is that they sell so that you don't have to. It gives people the comfort of being sold on you by looking at your material, being self-convinced that you are the expert, that you know what you're talking about. It's great! As a salesperson, whether you recruit or whether you sell life insurance, by the time people pick the phone up and call you, it's not a question of "Who are you? Is this a guy I can trust?" It becomes a matter of "OK, I'm sold on this agent, I'm sold on you. What's your recommendation?" Wouldn't you agree that you see the same process?*

JR: Yes. Absolutely. Even if you have a small amount of content on your website, it displays your expertise. People will see that you know what you are talking about. It's a no-brainer to have a website.

DD: *Let's talk about the consequences of not having a website. Where do you see an agent who doesn't invest time and resources into developing a web presence? What are the consequences long-term to their business?*

JR: There's no central hub for your business. There's not anywhere that a client, a referral, your upline, anybody, can come in and find information about you, learn more about you. That's the basic premise. It's a foundation for people to get to know you. If you don't have that, you're immediately losing trust. You'll lose on referrals not being able to check you out. That's what people do these days. I get a referral to somebody, I always Google them or go to the website and check them out. I don't care who it is, a realtor, a mortgage guy, anything. I'm going to check them out and learn about them.

Beyond that, you lose out on potential organic leads as well. I'll talk about this further into the interview. You're generating leads from search engines even if you don't have a lot of content. I have agents that have a 5 to 10-page website and they'll write a couple of applications a year from it organically. Somebody's searching in their area and they've shown up on a Google map. They'll get an inbound call. The consequences of not having a website are losing out on potential leads, losing trust from referrals, and losing out on a central hub for your business. You need to be out there and accessible to everyone. That's what your website does for you.

DD: Yes. The thing is that in insurance, the competition is stiff. It gets more so with each passing year. You have to be active. Do things to differentiate yourself. You have to sell yourself. More people now than ever before are doing their due diligence before they make an ultimate decision on buying something. They research online, figuring out who this person is and what they have to say. Are you credible or are you not? If you don't leverage that, you're missing out.

JR: Absolutely. You'll lose some sales to somebody who does have a website where people can learn more about them. If you have a website, you can display your expertise and build some trust with your clients. It happens all the time.

DD: I can hear some agents objecting, "Oh, it's the web. I don't know anything about the web. I'm an insurance salesperson. How do I even start with a website?" Could you describe the process to agents out there? What does it take to build a website? How simple really is it?

JR: There are two ways that you can get a website. You can own it or rent it. There are services out there where you can get a web presence, and it works. You pay around $40-$50 a month. There are dozens of them. But you never own your website. If you stop paying them, that website goes away. I don't recommend that route, but it is an easy way to at least start and get something out there. The second way is to own your website. We build our websites. I know you have websites on WordPress, Dave. It's so easy to learn. You can watch a 15 minute tutorial on YouTube, or Google it. Learn about WordPress.

Getting a website up on WordPress is easy and it's cheap. I build websites on selltermlife.com. It's one of our main services there. They're the same websites that we use to generate 10,000+ leads a month. It's so easy to get a website. It's so simple and it's so cheap.

DD: Yes, in this day and age. It was different 10-15 years ago. The web was in its infancy and coding was difficult. You had to know HTML. You don't need to know that anymore. You need to get on Youtube. There are tutorials there that are easy to follow. You can have your own website in a matter of minutes or hours. You're on the internet and you're in business.

JR: You can spend a few hours on your own, buying a host. They'll upload WordPress for you, upload a theme. You could spend a few hours doing it for less than $100 with ease.

DD: It is such a simplified process. Bottom line, there's no excuse. It's affordable. It's easy to do. The upside is tremendous.

Some people believe that the web is a pathway to developing business and being successful in insurance, but they look at it and think, "Well, geez, it's 2018. I didn't start, like Jeff did, back in 2009. I'm nine years behind. How could I even be competitive in an environment like this?" How can an insurance agent interested in doing this do it with success? Considering what's out there? With this perception of the competition that there is?

JR: There are lots of ways to go about it. If you can commit to at least one hour a day of either writing content or learning how to market online, that's all you need to do. Stick to it. Almost 95% of agents will give up in four months on their website, on even trying. They'll write content for four months and say, "Man, I haven't gotten a single lead yet!" There was a guy on my podcast who was getting over 500 leads a month, within 18 months, but he didn't get his first lead for this first three to four months. He didn't get daily leads for six to eight months. Writing content is prospecting. If you commit to it, it works. Let me give you an example of an agent who was on my podcast recently. He had over a thousand leads last month; final expense only. He totally committed to the program. There are other final expense agents out there doing the same thing, getting few leads a day from their website, and doing that within a year. That's what it takes. The difference between an agent with a successful website and an agent that's not getting any new business from the website is commitment and time. That's it. Sometimes you need a little bit more time.

A lot of agents don't have the runway to make that work. I know that you, Dave, work with a lot of agents that use direct mail, face to face. You have that engine going already. You spare an hour or two a day for your website. You write some content or learn how to do pay-per-click or paid marketing or something. You take some time to learn that, building that side of your business as well. We're both fishing from two different ponds. A direct mail lead is somebody completely different to a lead that goes online to look for final expense insurance. That area that you're in, you may be hitting them with direct mail, but there's also that group of people (I'm sure it's less than the direct mail group) that would go online. We get a lot of kids that want to buy final expense insurance for their parents. That's one market that most direct mail is missing. It's not that complicated. In order to do it with success, you need to commit to it. Put in the time. That's all it takes. The knowledge is out there.

DD: *I can understand people thinking, "Well, I'll write all these articles, I'll spend 6 months, 12 months, doing that and I might not be full time with leads coming in." One way to look at that, I'm sure you'd agree, is that that's the barrier to entry. As with everything in life, you have to have patience, you have to be committed, you have to write the articles, even when you don't want to. A lot of people won't do that. For those people that commit, like the gentleman you've mentioned, if they believe in the process, it will succeed. Imagine working from home in your underwear, never having to go out in the field again. It's a great thing for the people who stick with it.*

JR: Absolutely. It changes lives for sure to not have to worry about prospecting or buying leads. This is traffic coming to your website that you're not paying for. It means total freedom in this business if you can make that work.

DD: *What are the principles of success and marketing online and selling over the phone?*

JR: I always teach agents that there are four growth levers in your business. This will cover this question. I'll go through a few of them. Number one is lead acquisition. You can do search engine optimization (SEO) to your website. You can do direct mail. You can do pay-per-click, media buys, radio and TV. There are so many different ways to do it.

I'll go through the other three growth levers. You can pull any of these levers to be more profitable in your business. Lead acquisition is number one, lead conversion is number two. Know what you say, how you say it, what you're selling. It all has to do with lead conversion. Two agents may get the same 200 internet leads a month and one may make double that of the other. One may not even be profitable whilst the other may be very profitable. The lead acquisition is the same, but their lead conversion is pretty terrible. That's a training issue.

Number three is placements. I know that for final expense it is probably smaller than it is for term. We'd sell mostly term, fully underwritten, that kind of thing. Number four is retention and cross-selling. Most agents make a sale and they enjoy that deposit in their bank account, but they never do anything beyond that. They don't have a system in place to sell them something else that's up, whatever a final expense agent could sell them.

Focus on optimizing those four levers; lead acquisition, lead conversion, placement, and retention and cross-selling. It's not good enough to simply acquire the leads. We provide leads to our agents through a program. We can listen to the call, see how many dials they're making, everything. We know they're profitable. If an agent says, "These leads are horrible, I can't make these work," that's a training opportunity for lead conversion, placement, etc.

We've learned pretty fast that we can't just teach them how to generate leads, where to buy leads or anything like that. It has to do with lead conversion and placement. When I say retention and cross-sell, that's building a long-term value of a client. I don't know what the average premium is for final expense face to face. Let's say it's $700. If you can get that to $800 by selling something else to one out of every 10 people you sell, you could potentially outbid all your competitors online. You're making it worth more. Look at it that way. Don't focus solely on lead acquisition. At the same time focus on conversion placement and retention. Now you're on to something special.

A lot of agents want to focus on marketing. Some of them are great salespeople. They've nailed the script. They've nailed their presentation, they've nailed everything, but they don't have the right leads. The lead acquisition part is lacking. You have to have a good combination of all four of these to be really profitable in this business. It translates, not only to telesales, but I'm sure to the face to face market as well.

DD: Yes it does. I can speak especially to the value of developing a business. This is my seventh year in the business and I still learn from my mistakes. There's one thing that I've realized through self-analysis: What it takes to be successful in life insurance sales is patience. It's very easy to want to focus on leads and want to make that sale. Trust me, that's very important, but there's a lot of value, like you said, to taking that book of business and developing a clientele out of it. Develop a relationship, help them with other insurance needs that they have. If you do a good job on the front end then you're going to sell them other things, putting together programs that will raise your average ticket price per client. You can outbid your competitors in the market and do a fantastic job in the long-term. As in with developing a website that does well and generates organic leads, it's a patience thing. It always is in this businesses. You need to stay focused on developing that multi-year view.

JR: It's so important. I know that we're talking about generating leads and websites here, but I always have to slide that in there. It is very important in order to make all this work. Your lead acquisition doesn't mean anything if you can't do the back end of it.

DD: Back to talking about leads again. There are two different processes. There is the organic development of leads. That's where you write articles, rank for specific keywords in Google and people click on your website. It happens organically over time. The other process is the purchasing of leads, getting with a vendor or going on Facebook and doing a pay-per-click type of ad. Which is better? Under what circumstances would you recommend an agent to follow one path over the other?

JR: I have a lot of agents that do this part-time. They wait tables or have some other job. In that case, I'd say to take your time. Do the organic route because there is runway involved. You'll need some time to make that work. You can leave your job or do whatever you want once it starts pumping out enough leads. The number one thing for organic lead generation is that it needs runway. A lot of agents don't have that runway. Again, that's a barrier to entry. It's a reason why there's not a ton of sites out there doing well. That commitment level needs to be there over time.

I know you're asking me which one is better and the answer is that it depends. I'm a huge fan of organic traffic. It's free, money wise, obviously you invest your time in it. The most successful agents I see have some organic traffic in play.

A lot of people will start with paid. You buy leads, turn them for a profit, or you learn pay-per-click. I'll use a final expense campaign we have going on as an example. When I first started Facebook ads in final expense, I was generating leads for about $22 to $25 a lead. I would say, "OK, I see them being sold for $35 a lead in the open marketplace. I get it, the guy is making $10 a lead, cool, good business for him." Then I got down to $18 a lead. That took me two or three months. I wasn't bidding much. I was bidding $20, $25 a day and over time I got it down to $18 by switching up some ad sets etc. I was doing well for about five months. It's profitable, but now we have it down to the $9 to $11 mark. Incredible ROI. But it took me eight or nine months to figure that out. It does take some time, if you pay for traffic, if you do paid ads, media buying, all that. But it's scalable and that's the most important part.

Organic traffic scales over time, slowly, but paid traffic is completely scalable. The reason I like that over buying leads is that you're sending it to a website that you own. You tell them that you're calling from XYZ Final Expense, they immediately put that together with the form that they filled out on your website. With most internet leads, they don't know where you're calling from. Paid traffic is a better lead than purchasing a lead on the open market because you generate it yourself. There's that parallel between where they filled it out and where you're calling from. An agent can pursue paid traffic. It might take some time to optimize their campaigns but time is all that it takes. A lot of agents say pay-per-click doesn't work, Facebook ads don't work. They just didn't put enough time or energy into it.

I know you guys have a great entry point with fixed cost direct mail leads. It's a clear entry point for final expense. Some agents start generating a lead at $75 a week and then they think that this doesn't work. It takes time for organic leads that have an entry with direct mail. At the same time, to get true freedom in this business you need to have some sort of control, instead of buying from a third party. Generate your own leads somehow. It could be referrals, that is a great way to build. There's also organic traffic and paid traffic. The barrier to entry is there and it scares a lot of agents away, but it will give you freedom in this business, once you crack that code and figure that out. Then you'll never have to worry about where your next prospect is coming from. You don't have to worry about direct mail costs going up or their response rates going down in your area, or anything like that. To build that skill set is massive.

To answer your question, it doesn't matter. Organic or paid, it doesn't matter. Pick one, and go with it. But if there's something that's working, keep doing what you're doing while you explore this other side. That's what most agents are doing.

DD: When developing a web presence, how important is it to develop a niche within your website as opposed to just saying, 'Hey, I sell life insurance'?

JR: It's very important. The quickest traction that I'm seeing with agents who build websites is with those who niche down. Final expense is a great niche, but you can niche down even further online. This is only if you are going after organic leads, by the way. When I'm talking niche, the conversion rates are so much higher. For example, I have a website that focuses on multiple sclerosis, mutiplesclerosislifeinsurance.com. It's a super long URL, who would even go there? But that thing consistently generates 15 to 25 leads, depending on the time of year. We always write one, two, or more applications a month on that. It has 10 or 12 pages of content on it.

There are final expense agents that are focused just to sell guaranteed issue to people in their area. The leads are not plentiful, but they'll get a lead once every couple of months or so for a geographic area. What I'm saying is that if you niche down, it's easy to rank in the search engines. The leads that you do get convert much higher than a generic lead that was just searching for final expense, insurance, burial, insurance, whatever. Those leads are people who are just exploring; for information, for the cost, etc. But if you have somebody searching for burial insurance with COPD, this guy is interested. He wants it. He has COPD and he's worried that he won't be able to get it or it's going to be too cost prohibitive. If you niche down to that and write some articles around COPD and burial insurance or any other health conditions out there, you're going to get some traction. You're going to rank a lot quicker because there's not a lot of people going after that. They're going to see you as an expert in burial insurance and COPD, or whichever health conditions you pick. So niching down organically is huge. You can put together the ultimate guide for every health complication, even write a review on a policy. For example, they might have bought Gerber Life Insurance policy and they want to know if it's any good. They'll search for "Gerber Life Insurance reviews" to see if that's a good policy or not. They'll compare it and they'll see that AIG is a little bit better priced. That's what I mean by niching down. You're speaking direct with the person who was searching online. That's the power of it. A lot of agents will just write about final expense insurance and they don't get much traction. But if you can write some very niche articles and do some marketing towards those articles, you'll get some traction.

DD: Let's look at conversion. When we look at a website, what are the elements necessary to furnish that website with content that brings in people who are interested and also converts them?

JR: There are a lot of websites out there that have the logos of who they sell plastered all over them. All this stuff about me and just me. I'll tell you what I know right now. The goal is to get a visitor to your webpage to convert into a lead at a high percentage. The more simple you can make your webpage, the higher your conversions percentage goes. For example, rootfin.com. That stuff used to convert at about 1-2%. I've continually been researching, reading and learning about conversions. Now the site converts at about 6-7%. Same traffic. 100 visits used to get one to two leads, now they get six to seven leads. If you niche down, those conversions go even higher. That multiple sclerosis site converts at about 12-15% because it's so niche. It doesn't get a lot of traffic, but it converts very high. The visitors that visit that page, they'll fill out that form.

So you know, there are a few things. Number one that I've learned is a techie thing. You want a quote form. You want to give them something in return for them giving you the information. You're going to get a higher conversion if you have instant quotes on your website. I know that you would prefer your prospects not to see the instant quotes because they don't know what to quote themselves based on their health conditions. But it will get you a higher conversion. The whole goal is to have a conversation. So it doesn't matter. Put an instant quote at the top or on the sidebar of all your articles and let them see the quotes, that's fine. You're going to exchange your contact information. For that, you're going to speak with them anyway. You can let them know why they do, or most likely why they don't qualify for that quote that they saw there. You're doing that for the conversation.

There are some other techniques. A pop up which slides as they scroll down your page, that's huge. That is another 1% in conversion that you get. There are pieces to a website that will make it convert higher. That's why I build websites that sell term life. Not to plug what I'm doing, we do what we do because agents are getting websites out there. They are renting the websites, or they are doing their own WordPress and they're getting traffic. But they're only converting 1-2% of their visitors. Our websites convert on average around 5%. You can get it up stronger if your content and your user experience is better. There's definitely research you could do. There are more ways to get more people to visit your website and fill out forms on there. By default, ours are converting very high. The main sales point of why I do these websites is because it gives agents a better chance to generate leads.

DD: Do you have any final words on what it takes to be successful selling over the phone and utilizing the web for lead generation?

JR: I would say that there's a ton of knowledge out there. The one thing that I see with agents who become successful is that they're resourceful. Let's say you don't have a website right now. If you're resourceful enough to go to YouTube, you could learn about WordPress and how to do a WP blog. About how to post something on that blog. Further than that, agents that have websites, they're figuring things out on their own. If you're resourceful, you're right for building a website. If you think you're going to need a mentor to see you through the entire way, you could still get a website, but I wouldn't advise you to market online. You need to be resourceful. That's the common denominator of a lot of agents who are being resourceful enough, beyond the commitment and the time they put into it, to get the answers themselves.

DD: Well, Jeff, I want to thank you so much for joining us today. Again, I want to plug Jeff's book here. 'The Digital Life Insurance Agent' book. You can find it on Amazon.com. Agents are going to be interested in learning more about your website design services as well as your podcast work, Jeff. Why don't you go ahead and remind us about that?

JR: Well, that's over at selltermlife.com. In the book, I talk a lot about this stuff. I go in depth about how to generate leads, that's why I wrote it. You'll know exactly what to do. If you get a website, the book will tell you the different paths you can go down to generate leads. Selltermlife.com has that podcast and that website service as well. You actually have an interview on that podcast as well, so you can listen to that also.

How To Sell Final Expense Over The Phone

Interview With Cody Askins Of Secure Agent Mentor

About Cody Askins

If you're looking to get into telephonic sales, you will need somebody who knows how to do it well.

We're going to go into a deep dive on how to sell final expense and Cody's experience in the business. More specifically we will be talking about final expense telesales.

DD: Let's start from the top. Can you tell us a little bit about yourself, how you got into the insurance business, and what you're doing today?

CA: I own and run Secure Agent Mentor. I actually grew up in the business. My Dad's been in the business 28 years now. As a kid, I never thought I would want to get into it. I thought, "It's insurance. I don't want to get into it!" But I did. I got into insurance at Mutual of Omaha. I was there as an intern at 17, 18, years old. I got to where I enjoyed it. I went part-time in the business for a little bit, then at 19, I was in college playing basketball. I went full time and was fortunate enough to make $117,000 in a very short time and I fell in love. I became obsessed. I absolutely loved this business.

When you're a captive agent at a lot of these agencies, as I was, telesales is a curse word. You do not do that. Don't quote, don't help qualify, get in the home. The old spiel. Especially with all the old-fashioned guys in this business. But I always knew that I wanted to get into training and marketing. That's where my bigger passion lies.

I did well at Mutual, then we went out and started our own brokerage. We created a call center. I sold my share of that call center about three years ago and then this year I started another call center. I love it, I've always enjoyed telesales. The main reason why is that I don't like to drive, as crazy as that sounds. I live in southwest Missouri. If I leave Springfield (and it's not big, it's around 50,000 people), I've got to drive at least an hour, maybe two. I'm in the middle of the state. There's nothing close once you get outside of Springfield. So I got into telesales and now I do all kinds of stuff.

DD: It's funny that you mentioned that about driving. As a rule, I train face to face with guys myself. One of the things that they like is the driving. That delineates what kind of agent does better in certain environments. It's funny how a lot of guys, when I talk to them, they say, "I can't imagine being chained to my desk!" Then again, if you're doing well, you won't much care!

CA: One of my buddies here in the office in Dallas, he loves to drive. We used to drive all over the state together door knocking everywhere. I would say, "You can drive. I'll hang out in the passenger seat!"

DD: As you got into your Mutual of Omaha career, you were a captive agent. You sold the traditional route, you sold their life insurance products to people. Eventually, you transitioned to this call center, this telephonic sales environment. What process did you go through to get to the point of getting into the call center environment, selling it over the phone?

CA: I've always been a natural born salesperson. That's what separates me, face to face or over the phone. How I connect with people. I put on a big old smile, I build a relationship, I build rapport. That's why I've always excelled. It's becoming a friend first, then the sale comes. I issued myself a challenge to do telesales. I was always told that it's bad over the phone. That I didn't want to do it, it's difficult. You know what? It isn't easy, by any means. But I always knew that I could write more policies once I got on the independent side of the business. I started to hear of all these big call centers selling thousands of policies a year. I'm crazy, so I think I can do that. I started focusing on teleselling, improving, listening to audiobooks, listening to videos. I met people, interviewed people. I'm better at telesales now than I ever was at field sales, which I never thought I'd be able to say.

DD: You're saying that you weren't like that in the beginning? That this is a process of training and learning and adjusting as you go on?

CA: It's funny you mentioned that. We had a final expense and Medicare Supplement call center. This was back in March of 2015. There were four partners in this, and three agents. Three closers taking transfers from openers. I was only doing the closing and applications, etc. I wasn't doing the initial calls. Our very first month teleselling we made nine sales. Nine sales. I wasn't going to stop there! Before we knew it, by June of that same year, only a few months later, we're doing 60 or 70 apps a month. We had no sales experience, no insurance experience. We were all at Mutual of Omaha together. No telesales experience. No one knew what the freak they were doing. We were determined to figure it out. A lot of times that's all you need.

DD: If there's a will, there's a way. A lot of what I'm doing these days is reviewing. I read the literature from the classic salespeople in the insurance business. The thing that I see a lot is that the most successful people had periods of time where they struggled. Sometimes for many years. Look at Ben Feldman or John Savage. These guys were mediocre for the best part of a decade before they got anywhere. You have to have an element of faith. Even if you don't know what you're doing. Have the willpower and the capability to learn from your mistakes and improve upon them. That's the only way you can go. Eventually, you're going to get it right. That's how I've always looked at it.

CA: Exactly. Figure something out. Put your mind to it long enough and work at it, whether it's field sales, telesales, or sales in general. There's often a struggle before you hear about that awesome story, that awesome week. That's how this world is.

DD: *It's so true in business. There was a guy, a home builder, in a BNI group with me about five years ago. He had been in home building for 30 years. He built middle-class homes, nothing fancy. He landed a deal for a custom-designed building. The client had made a ton of money, millions of dollars. He was building a house worth at least $15,000,000 in Tennessee. It was a ridiculous mansion. He said to us, "I'm an overnight success after 30 years."*

I understand that. People don't see the past. They ask, "Wow, how'd you get this client? You're making millions of dollars off of doing this deal!" There's a lot that goes into it that very few people realize. Nobody's ever interested in hearing about it. That's a life lesson for any salespeople or business owners. You have to pay your dues.

CA: All those behind the scenes late hours that you and I and others put in, sooner or later, they pay off. 92% of insurance agents fail in their first three years. Those that make it, they endure some struggles but they keep the faith. They work hard and in the end it pays off. That's why this business is so lucrative. It can be so freaking rewarding. That's another reason why I love it.

DD: *It's true. It was either John Savage or Al Granum that said, "If you just last, you'll make it. If you can just survive." Of course, with learning from your lessons. I think it was also one of the two that said, "When you start the insurance business, it's like a four-year degree." You're not going to go to college and make $200,000 a year as a general physician. At medical school, you will make $20,000, $30,000, a year. You will do residency work. It will suck. They will try to get you to quit. You will have to deal with all sorts of people, work all nights. You're a slave. When you make it, then you're making that kind of money. In reality, that's how the insurance business is. A lot of the guys that get great at it struggle that first couple of years. It's having that faith and consistency to stick with it despite* *that. No matter what everybody else is telling you to do; to quit, go get a real job, etc.*

Why don't we jump into telesales? A lot of people reading this are face to face agents, as indeed most insurance agents are. When they think about telesales, they ask, "How is that even possible? How can you collect personal information? How can you overcome the trust barriers? How can you stand sitting in front of a desk all day?"

Let's dive right in. What are the big differences between a face to face agent selling any kind of life insurance versus the one that sells over the phone? What are the differences in their selling technique? What does it take to succeed in selling over the phone versus face to face?

CA: It takes a lot more time and a lot more work, although you can get that on both sides. The biggest difference is that it takes a lot more leads, a lot more contacts, talking to a lot more people. There are so many agents that think that it's nigh on impossible. I get agents right now, even to this day that say, "There are carriers that allow you to sell on the phone?"

There are myths: You sell smaller cases. Your retention is worse. You won't sell as many cases. We'll get into that. I'll get some numbers for you. Agents fail in person because they don't run enough appointments. Agents fail in telesales because they don't talk to enough people. That's the main thing. You're not going to tell everyone how great they are, how awesome they are at building rapport. It's a numbers game. If you don't talk to enough people, you won't make enough money. I bet 99.5% of agents would fail if they only focused on telesales. The reason that 92% of all agents fail is that is it's hard to get in front of enough people in person. How much harder is it to talk to enough interested, qualified people that you can turn into a sale over the phone? It's natural that you'd need a lot more. Those agents have never talked to enough people to actually succeed over the phone. Or they think that price is all that matters and they sell price. The relationship, the time you spend with the clients, still trumps price as much it does in the field. They ignore that fact.

DD: You know me, I'm not a telesales guy. This is all an education for me as much as for the next guy. I know several successful agencies down around Mississippi that have 10 or 20 agents. They do telemarketing leads, that kind of thing. They're the big call centers. Do you think that it's better for an agent who's going to do telesales to work in a call center environment? One thing that I've not seen a lot, and I'd like your thoughts on, is an agent on their own, in their own home. How successful do you think they can be at home, with a system or a setup something like you teach?

CA: That's a great question. It's so difficult to know what to do to have the right training, have enough leads. We have the training. We have the leads, we can help with all that. It's much easier to succeed if you go sit in a call center like ours, or any of these monster centers across the country. There, you can sit and sell over the phone and get paid a much smaller commission.

I want control. That's my personality. I want to know what's going on, I want to own it. I don't want to go and be someone's kid sitting in a call center. Them telling me what to do. Only getting a small piece of the pie. I want the whole freaking pie.

Not everyone's like that. It takes a certain personality and drive to want to do it on your own. You've got to realize that, as in field sales, there's investment. There's a bigger investment to telesales. It's possible to sell over the phone by cold calling in 2018, but it's extremely difficult. You'd have to have so many openers, cold calling, transferring calls to you. At the end of the day, it's much smarter to be talking to interesting people and then qualifying them. Then you're only talking to them when they can answer the health questions. They're not GI, they have a bank account, they actually have interest, etc. You flip it on its head. Most people think they need to talk to a ton of people as a closer. Telesales works best when you've got an opener closer model. You're splitting up the responsibilities. As that closer, you are talking to 10, 12, 15 people a day or more that are qualified and have interest. Then you spend time with those.

DD: *A lot of people think, "Hey, I've got to make the calls cold, or with leads, I have to do the whole pitch, from start to finish." It sounds like you endorse, and do, something different. Can you go into that model a little bit more? To whatever level you're comfortable with? How do you work and how do you suggest it should work?*

CA: I don't mind being transparent about everything. It doesn't bother me at all. It's not easy to do telesales. I could give away all my secrets and there there's no guarantee that anyone would succeed. Agents think, "I can just get on the phone and cold call. I'll call paid leads, I'll call 30 new leads a week. I can make it, I can succeed."

You can, but it's the toughest way to do it. You have to spend all your time doing the $10 an hour work that could be delegated. People are spending 90% of their time trying to find that qualified, interested, person. Only 5% or 10% of their time is spent closing. Let's flip that on its head. Delegate that work to someone else. Spend 90%, 95% of your time talking to interested qualified individuals. It's the best model for telesales and most places still don't do that, don't realize it. The best way, in my experience, is to have leads flowing into a dialer. Using a predictive dialer. Calling one, two, three numbers at a time. Our call center dials two numbers at a time. It's not even that big, and we do 80 to 100 final expense apps per month over the phone. Some weeks more than 20, some weeks less than 20. We have two openers transferring to four closers. If you have enough lead flow and you're using a dialer, they're talking to someone every 30 or 60 seconds. They're reading a script. They're pre-qualifying the person. The opener is there, making sure that they can qualify, they're not GI, they have a bank account. They're asking everything needed. Once the client meets all the qualifications, then they transfer them to a closer. People think that they need two or three openers for every one closer they're transferring to. If you're using leads and a dialer, it's actually the opposite. One good opener can keep two to three closers busy full time if you're doing it right.

This surprises most people. They say, "That doesn't make any sense. That's crazy!" But that's the math and it's true. That's the best way that it works. We have two openers transferring to three closers and our call center manager. It's a small operation. We started up a few months ago and already we're starting to add a person a week. We're starting to scale it up, now that we have figured out and perfected the exact numbers of it. I've got so much going on that I'm not looking to have a thousand man call center. If I can, one day, write 1,000, 2,000, 5,000 final expense apps a year, in a small operation, that's a start.

DD: It makes a lot of sense. As a face to face agent, one of the best ways to leverage your time is to hire someone to set the appointments for you to go on. It's better than travailing the countryside and trying to find if somebody is home or not. Not to say that it's a bad method to do that. It's great. But you can be much more efficient, for a very affordable price. For the price of one policy commission a week, get booked with a bunch of appointments and have your life back. You don't have to sit down in front of the phone between 6 pm and 9 pm to get booked for the following day. There are people who will take $10 an hour, give or take, to do this for you.

CA: We start our openers out at $8 an hour, with a little bonus for when they transfer a sale to us. Our closers can choose, either hourly plus a small commission or a piece of the larger dimension by going 100% commission. Agents out there that don't want to hire someone for $400 a week, you can still go to www.onlinejobs.ph. Get a Filipino telemarketer. Start with one or two, spend $60, $80, $100, $120. Throw some paid leads into a dialer and at least start to learn the system. It's not perfect. I mean this well, a lot of times there's some broken English. But they're able to transfer calls to you and you're able to talk to people. It's not ideal, but it's a start. It gets you on the phone. You're still delegating some of that weeding out. You're only talking to qualified, interested individuals that have time for you. They have a checking account, they are healthy enough to talk to you.

This will surprise people. We only write guaranteed issue business when we've got a spouse applying for a health policy or a day one policy. Otherwise, we try not to because of the amount of time it takes and the little return. They get the policy in the mail, they see the two-year wait, or the fact that United of Omaha's direct consumer GI is crazy. They're dismayed. We don't want to get into that business. I always try to focus on quality. Our closers are on 100% commission, or $10, $11 an hour plus a small commission. Their time is best suited talking to someone that can give us the best ROI.

DD: Let's go through the process of qualifying these people. Your openers have established the criteria that you're looking for. That will suit and, like you said, be a good use of your closer's time. You get the closer on the phone with them, they do what they need to do. What are the most common two or three objections, for example? Most people reading this are face to face. They get certain kinds of objections. They think that there would be objections about personal information and banking information. What kind of objections do you experience as a telesales agent and how do you guys overcome them?

CA: We try to train our staff to handle those as well as we can. Most salespeople want to handle objections at the end of the call or on the close. If an objection is going to come up, I want to get it out as early as I can, in the first 10, 15, 20 minutes. I don't want to go over benefits and talk about value and get into price until I know that they're going to make a decision. Until I'm confident that when I ask them, "Which of these three are you most comfortable with?" they're going to make a decision.

Price isn't much of an objection we get, believe it or not. The main objections are trust related. "I don't know you, I don't trust you, I'm on the phone." They don't say, "I don't like you," but I like to throw that in sometimes, just for fun!

That's why we take our time. Our average sale takes over an hour because I don't want to sell price. I can spend 10, 15, 20 minutes on this on the phone, but I don't want to. We've got a script. We have five, six, seven pages of initial script. We spend 20, 30 minutes building rapport, building trust. We're trying to overcome any trust objections they may have. We always use phrases like, "Hey, we've got a thousand clients who said the exact same thing and I'm with you." Then they take that leap of faith, once they know that we are who we say we are. That they're doing business with someone in their state. It makes all the sense in the world and they're happy. We have a lot of awesome, happy customers!

To put them in that frame of mind, we can send them to a website, we can have them call our office. We can text them a picture of our insurance license. I have even got as crazy as texting a picture of my driver's license. I don't care, anything that we can do to gain that initial trust. Be creative and do some little things.

It comes down to time. Building rapport, taking our time. Those agents that think they're selling price, that price is most important? What they're going to sell are little bitty, dinky cases that don't stick on the books, I can promise you. They're selling based on price and they're not spending enough time with the prospect.

DD: You have the capability and the leverage to use these supplementary things. Showing your license, your website, your office, you in person, that's great. I'm curious; for what percentage of your sales or one call closes are you having to do multiple callbacks? Is it commonplace to have that happen?

CA: A little bit. We've got one closer that allows people to call people back. I would say about 80% is on the first call. I won't call anybody back and I try to get my call center manager to get that transfer down to my closers and openers. But sometimes it's a one-legged call. There are little things that we can't always overcome. There's a certain clientele that won't always make a decision on the first call. We will call them if we think they are truly serious and there's a great chance to make the sale. I won't call them back for a $20, $30 a month sale, that's not going to happen. Generally, they're making that decision on their own. They can make the decision right there anyway. Some people want to think about it, they want to talk to their spouse, they want us to call them back. We won't allow it to happen unless we're calling them back within 24 hours and it's scheduled. Otherwise, they're going to forget. It's a waste of time. We need to figure out a way to overcome that objection. Take a little more time. We don't have to call back as much as people think. We focus on the one call close. It doesn't feel like we're closing them, but that's what we focus on.

DD: *Related to that, you guys aren't cold calling. If you're using paid leads of some type, how willing would you be to talk about what you use? What would you suggest agents use, as far as leads that would work well with telesales? What kind of leads aren't the best?*

CA: I would flip that on its head and say that we don't use direct mail. A lot of agents use direct mail in person. Our main sources are our online digital leads, social media advertising, Facebook, Instagram, Google etc. Also some telemarketing. People are used to answering the phone. The only thing to get into there is guaranteed issue. You need a lot. We prefer digital leads, online leads. I'm not going to NetQuote, Precise, or Life Leads Direct and buying Internet leads. I would go home with one in twenty. It's a nightmare. We're focusing on generating our own leads through online, digital advertising, and supplementing them with some telemarketing.

DD: *What you're saying is the old adage in final expense. Direct mail is king for face to face agents. I can assume some reasons why you would do digital leads. What do you think makes your digital lead creation better than direct mail for telesales?*

CA: We can call them in real time. We can call them within 24 hours. We don't have to pay near the cost of direct mail. We don't have to wait weeks to make the call. Nowadays, I've got a better chance of my digital lead being exclusive than my direct mail or telemarketing. I prefer that. Those customers are also a little more tech savvy, online savvy. They're more likely to buy over the phone. They're used to doing business through websites and social media. They have a phone, they have internet, a computer, an email address, Facebook. All those little things that actually help our main objective.

DD: *You're spot on. Final expense clients are traditionally people who are at home watching TV. They've got a flip phone, they're not on Facebook, not online. They've spent their entire life replying back to direct mail cards. That is how they are by design and they'll continue to send these cards back.*

That's what most of them do. But, as you know, there's this growing market who are now on Facebook, using the internet. They have changed how they buy. It seems to me that the people sending direct mail that want final expense, they want face to face. The buyers want a face to face appointment. That's how they've always bought.

Now we also have this digital market, I see that as a growing trend over the next 10 to 20 years in final expense. Final expense is one of the laggers in catching up with technology. The digital market is used to doing the research. They're used to being able to access the internet and qualify who you are, your website, and answer those particular objections. They actually prefer it. I, for example, haven't had a salesperson in my home for over 10 years. If somebody comes knocking, even though I sell face to face, I don't let them in. It's very rare for me to give somebody the opportunity for a pitch.

CA: I do the exact same thing. I don't let anybody that I don't know personally into my home, yet I've got agents that are in people's homes every day, door knocking, cold calling. Maybe that demographic is more likely to let them in. It's true, the digital market is expanding. I like that type of lead. It's a little more educated about what's going on online.

DD: The other thing that you get with digital leads is an email address. If they're online, they've got an email. They are using their smartphones. You can text them. Looking from the outside in, you've got so many more opportunities to contact these people. To drip on them over time, even if they don't buy. To automate that whole process. That's the biggest problem with a face to face environment. You don't have any of that. You have to pay the old-fashioned way. You have to do a direct mail. It's more expensive. Sure, it works, but it's a lot cheaper, as you said, to develop leads online, and you get their contact information. Is that a tremendous help in gaining their trust so as to make the sales?

CA: It is. Another thing that a lot of a lot of call centers will use is TV leads. We've tinkered with them a little, buying them from the TV lead vendor. Not running our own commercials. But the cost of TV leads is a lot more than it used to be. As usual with final expense or insurance, everyone started to hear about this thing that's working, then they all started to run towards it. It's how it works. The TV lead is also generally in a little worse health. They're sitting in front of the TV. They're sitting by the phone. We've used that a little, but digital is king for what we do. That's what we prefer.

DD: That makes perfect sense. I advocate direct mail for the face to face guy. It's the best way to do business. It's undeniable that it's what most agents do. However, there's no way that prices for postage can stay as low as they are. They will be suppressed for as long as they are subsidized. Postage should be triple what is paid. We've seen a huge upsurge in this business as a result of the failure of business models of health insurance. More people are doing final expense face to face. A lot of people are leaving Medicare Advantage and getting into this. They are all doing the same thing. Mildred is now getting six or eight direct mails a month, and she's only going to reply to one or two. That particular segment is so competitive. There are markets that we work in where you cannot get a lead at an affordable rate with direct mail.

CA: That's 100% true. You know that specific type of lead and that part of the industry as well as anybody that I know.

DD: It's an unfortunate reality that we all have to contend with if we're going to do face to face sales. Some markets are fine, but I can't go into a lot of the more traditional areas to sell final expense face to face. I'd love the work, but I'd pay $50 or 6$0 bucks a lead. For final expense, it's crazy. Do you have a preference in marketplaces? Where do you target for final expense telephonic sales? Do you target areas that are more metropolitan? Or more rural, smaller, upper midwestern states, those small populations? What kind of strategy, if any, do you guys employ?

CA: Even for someone face to face, those metro areas are high target areas. They're getting the most calls, the most mail. It's easier to target those. We target all areas the same, but we prefer a rural individual. They're talking to fewer people, getting less mail. They're two hours from the nearest insurance agent. They might be getting fewer phone calls or they're on the 'do not call' list. That helps. We prefer rural. But we get a lot more metro.

DD: There's only so many people that live in a rural area. As much as you'd like to work it, you have to mix it in with some metro. I like working in Van Buren county, up the road from me, but there are only around 900 people between 50 and 80 that live there! I'll get ten leads there if I'm lucky.

I've heard about the challenge that you did. You wrote in excess of $40,000. Was it only life premium, final expense, or a mixture of those? I'd like you to describe what that was all about. Can you go into detail for people that are curious, that would like to look at more about that?

CA: We have a Hundred Day Challenge page on our site, where we can talk about it. In 35 days I did 100 apps. Mixed: some terms, some non-med, some fully underwritten. I'd take whatever I could get. The majority was final expense. That was the target. The total premium was a little over $65,000. In 35 days, over the phone. Only me, closing all of them. I did that because I get so many agents that think telesales is impossible. They email, text, or call and say, "I would love for you to bring light to telesales and how possible it is."

Yes, it's tougher than field sales. But my marketing team and I, we brainstorm. We meet every morning. I meet with my call center owner and managers, my agency director, and my marketing team. I come up with wild, crazy ideas daily somehow, as I'm sure that you do. We get creative and our minds get to turn. One day I said, "You know what would be nuts? 100 apps in 100 days." It would be nuts because I stay busy. I like to stay very busy, as I'm sure you do. "You know what? That's not bad. What about $100,000? That's pretty good, but it's still a hundred days. Let's call it the Hundred Day Challenge. You do a hundred apps as fast as you can, just to bring light to telesales."

So I did the same as I do in the call center. Leads into a dialer, openers transferring to me. Setting up call back appointments to the point where I'm talking to 15, 20 people a day. I had to put everything else on hold and do some delegating that I wouldn't normally do during that time. We recorded a lot of these challenge calls. We were doing a transition in software in my call center, so for the last half, I wanted to speed it up. It was taking too long, so I went and sat in my call center and let them transfer me calls. I had to get this thing over with as soon as I could. It was a ton of fun. It was a monster challenge. I don't want to do it again right now at all because it was all day, every day, 12, 13 hours a day. But it was fun. It brought a lot of attention to telesales and what it's possible to achieve.

My agency director, he has agents ask, "I want to sell over the phone, what can I do to do that?"

"Cody's got a lot of experience in this. He focuses," he has to explain. "Before he even gets into benefits, he spends 45, 50 minutes building value. He does all his trial closes an hour before he even gets into the price."

You have to focus on building rapport. Spend a lot of time on it. Most people don't understand all that. They don't realize that it took a lot of leads. It took a system, it took a lot of experience. It took an opener, it took some dialers. I had to invest a lot of money in a short amount of time. It took a lot of my time. It's not something that anyone can jump in and do.

***DD:** The challenge you did was fantastic. There's a level of selling that you have to do in convincing these guys that it's possible. We're all doubting Thomases, we have to see it to believe it. You've got recordings. You've got training on how else could you better position yourself and the sale process. If you asked me two years ago if you can be successful in final expense telesales, I'd say. "Probably not. I don't know a lot of producers that have success." Now, I've had some experience with meeting other people doing this. I'm persuaded that there are some people that are better situated to sell over the phone, and there are those who are better situated going face to face. I've met a lot of people: yourself, others. There's a guy down in Kansas City who does telesales. He has all direct mail leads. He sells everything. He even mails the applications, he's so antiquated.*

CA: Gosh, I can't imagine mailing apps.

***DD:** I assume he does. The carrier whose convention I was on with him does not have a telephonic application nor an e-app. So the only way is the* *physical way. This guy was doing $200,000+ with this one carrier and I know he had other carriers also. That's amazing. Now I'm of the persuasion that you can be successful either way. You have to find the approach that best suits your personality. Do something that you enjoy doing. You don't enjoy driving. That's a driver to not go face to face. The same concept applies to the face to face guys.*

CA: I was focusing on writing as many apps as I could. But it's the same as field sales. Some of them will fall off. Some will get declined after they're submitted. Someone will change their mind. For you to try to do this from home, if you're doing it on your own, without an opener, without dialers, you need 50 to 100 leads a week. Just to do five sales. Sometimes more, sometimes less. For the first several weeks you're getting to know it. You're learning it. You think that your premiums are going to average $30, $40? Over the last several weeks, in my call center, our average monthly premium is $63.08. That's higher than my field agents.

DD: *That's better than my average face to face. I've seen guys that do telesales that seemed to have pretty good case sizes. In my experience, the average for doing it over the phone is not detrimental.*

CA: It's all about the way you do it. I tell all of our field agents, "Don't sell with your own pocketbook, your own wallet. You're not buying the product, they are." Focus on building rapport, building value. Propose what you think they need. Give them three options in descending order, not ascending order. Then they're more likely to choose the larger option.

DD: *Cody, what are your final thoughts? What tips do you have for the aspiring agent that wants to get into telesales? What would you tell them they need to do to succeed? What is your general advice for being successful in this type of business?*

CA: I would say the first thing is to record every single call. Especially if you're trying to do this on your own. That's the fastest way to learn what you're doing. We've all got bad habits. Things that we do, things that we say. I'm picky about that kind of stuff, so I try not to have them. But we all do. It's natural. If you can, listen to yourself and plug yourself into a script or a program, something that's working. Then record every call so that you can dissect and diagnose it. What you're doing well, what you're poor at doing. What you should be improving at. When you should be speaking, when you should be shutting up instead of speaking. When you're not speaking and should be. All those little things that we can learn from ourselves.

For instance, there's a lot of times where agents want to speak. They'll interrupt people. In telesales, especially if they are talking more than the prospect, I can tell you, they will not make that sale. We want to be listening more than we're talking. We're going to be asking open-ended questions. There's a couple of things that happen in telesales. At the beginning of the call, you've got to focus on building rapport, getting them to talk. But there are also those individuals that say, "What's the price?" If you give them the price when they're asking, when you're not ready to give it to them, the interview is over. You won't make the sale. They're shopping. They're not serious. They want you to regurgitate information so they don't need you anymore.

"I promise I'll get to that," I'll tell them. "Just give me a few more minutes to get to know you so I can give you the best possible price."

"No, I want the price now."

"I'm sorry, Mr. Jones, I want you to wait around and get it from me. I can't give you a price that's not perfect for you. It wouldn't make any sense."

I'll hang up on someone, tell them "Unfortunately, I have a lot of other people that I've got to get to." I'll move on before I regurgitate a price and then they don't buy.

DD: *Those are excellent tips, especially the recording one. It's good for any insurance agent, and especially important for the telephonic guy. All he has is his voice, his tonality, how he says things. He can't rely on body language.*

Cody, we are wrapping up our great interview today. For anybody that's interested in that position, how can people find you if they're interested in selling over the phone? Where can they find you?

CA: Go to www.secureagentmentor.com. We've rebuilt, rebranded, and spent a lot of money improving our site. Also, look for Secure Agent Mentor on Youtube, and www.facebook.com/secureagentmentor.

We've got a free Facebook group for agents, or they can always call our office 4178839300. Send an email to support@secureagentmentor.com. We'd love to help. David, you help a ton of agents and you do an awesome job of providing valuable content. We hope to do that as well.

How To Specialize In Selling Disability Insurance

Interview with Larry Schneider

About Larry Schneider

Larry is a disability insurance specialist with over 45 years of experience exclusively specializing in disability insurance. Larry has had published over 50 disability insurance related articles in many trade magazines. He has lectured for many leading associations and CPAs and has appeared on television explaining the contractual differences between policies offered by the insurance industry. He has also been a panelist for litigation conference. In addition, he is an expert witness consultant for disability insurance claims which were inappropriately denied, and a national resource for hard to place insurance applicants and application of business and individual standard cases.

Larry is also the author of a nationally acclaimed training manual, 'Encyclopedia Of Disability Income Insurance Manual' and the 'Anatomy Of Denied Disability Insurance Claims Manual', both of which are used by many attorneys, and will make an agent an overnight expert! I definitely recommend the Encyclopedia Of Disability Income Insurance Manual. Larry has also helped the American College substantially to rewrite their 'Essentials Of

Disability Income Insurance Manual'. He has also been a guest speaker at the MDRT 2013 convention and for many webinars. Before his insurance career, Larry headed a department for one of the big eight CPA firms performing analytical studies on behalf of their clients. Welcome to the interview.

LS: My pleasure. Thank you.

DD: Let's start from the top. Tell us a little bit about yourself and how you got into the insurance business.

LS: As you indicated, I was a management consultant for one of the big eight CPA firms whereby I was instrumental in bringing in new business. Over the years, it morphed into a thought that maybe I could sell and make more money, even though I was making a good income at that time. Then, I saw an advertisement in the newspaper which talked about insurance which said, 'Own Your Own Business. No capital required.' I went to one of the meetings which was about making money by selling disability insurance. Over a period of time, after attending many meetings and seeing the commission checks being handled, I realized maybe there's something to it.

So, we joined forces. I memorized their half an hour presentation and started to sell for the company and thereafter I became a partner. For 16 straight months I was a national sales leader and not knowing anything about it beforehand. The company was great in training and I became a trainer for the company sharing my experiences. That's how I got into the business. That was at age 39.

DD: This part of the conversation with you is directed towards the newer agents who are trying to figure out what type of insurance line they want to represent. Can you think of the new agent in mind and describe to them how selling disability insurance works in general and why? Why would a client want to buy it?

LS: Traditionally in the American mindset, life insurance has always been part of their inventory. Everybody knows that something's going to happen at some point in time. It could be sooner or later. With disability insurance, one has to create the need. It's a different method of selling because most of the prospects you call on usually say that nothing is going to happen to them and they don't need it. So, it's an emotional sale and you have to show reasons instead of saying they just need it. There is plenty of information out there which will help convert the non-believer into a believer.

I want to emphasize - and this is the genesis of selling disability insurance - that you have to present case studies of people who thought they would never need income protection, but all of a sudden they found out after taking the policy how useful it really can be. Just yesterday, the wife of one of my clients called and she said her husband fell off the ladder. She was initially against the insurance when he first took it out, but being a responsible person, he wanted it. I say to a lot of prospects when we finally shake hands one way or the other, that it's the biggest waste of money in the world, until you have to use it. Commission wise, most carriers pay 50% for the first year and typically 10% thereafter, even for a lifetime. It's not a bad way to develop a nice a retirement program.

DD: Larry, you made a good point a moment ago. You said disability is something that can happen more than people imagine. However, it's not necessarily going to happen. So when you say you need to create the need, you absolutely need to. What do you think?

LS: Absolutely. Clearly there are more people in the hospitals than in the funeral home at any given time. So the evidence is very strong and there are published statistics to support the need.

DD: You mentioned that disability has a pretty good first year commission, and case sizes can be very large. Plus it's a high renewal driven business. Is that how the product is?

LS: Absolutely. Even if you sell one policy a week with a premium of $2,000, that's $50,000 a year. In the second year you get 10% on $1,000. So in the second year again by selling just one policy week you made $51,000. But let's face it, the average agent does not sell just one policy a week. By the time the agent gets in the second year, he should be on a roll. If you do a good job like in any kind of business, you get referrals and you become stronger and more knowledgeable. Knowledge is power. The more power you have, the more successful you're going to be.

DD: How much is quality related to persistency? To new agents, persistency means the business must stick on the books. What kind of quality can you expect from the disability? How long does it last?

LS: Based on my 45 years experience selling disability insurance, there have been hardly any lapses other than those for retirement, when the people don't need it anymore.

Once on the books, even in the worst case scenarios lapses do not happen. For example, in an economic downfall when the prospect says that they can't afford it, there are ways to salvage that kind of situation. If income has gone down, there are ways to bring down the premium so that people can still maintain coverage on a lesser basis. Rarely is the insurance dropped either through competition or otherwise, simply because everybody knows that cost will increase over the years if a replacement is being discussed. Everything is based on age. I always try to offer the best from the industry and I represent all the insurance companies at this point in time. There are only about 13 carriers that currently remain in the insurance disability insurance industry. If another agent came in and said he had something better, he would face the challenge of overcoming the cost which would have increased due to age.

DD: The new agents may think that disability is complex, especially if they have seen the different kinds of policies that are available to prospects. Can you describe in general how disability insurance works and what the most common policies are? How should they go to work for a client when a disability claim comes in?

LS: You don't want to become a feature preacher. In 99% of cases, it's going to go over the prospect's head. What you want to do is create the need - what is the policy going to do for the client if they become disabled. It will give them a tax free income, money so they can pay their rent, their food and so on. To answer your question directly, the genesis of any policy is the definition of total disability. The policy also has many options available when applied for.

The different definitions of total disability are based on occupation and definitions trigger the benefit. For example, a ditch digger is not going to get the same definition of total disability as a doctor.

For a doctor, the definition would usually state, "Unable to do the material and substantial duties of your occupation". You can add an explanation which says, "Even though you're working in another occupation, making more money". For example, if somebody in sales loses his voice and can't do the duties of his occupation e.g. communicate, he/she would still get the full benefit from the policy. If it was paid for with after-tax dollars, then the benefits will be tax free. Another option is referred to as partial or residual. Let's say someone hurt their back and they couldn't work two out of five of the days... two out of five is 40% of the week and so they lose 40% of their income. The policy would then pay 40% of the monthly benefit on what they call a residual or a proportion of loss of income.

Another important option is referred to as a 'Future increase Option'. Let's say somebody didn't take out as much as they needed initially, or they got the most they could get based on their income at that time, but their needs or their income is going to increase dramatically in the next five years. The future increase option will give more coverage with no medical questions asked. So, if they've had some major health issues (which are overlooked), all they have to do to get an additional benefit through the future increase option is to prove that they have the financial income.

Another option is the cost of living adjustment. Once somebody is collecting the monthly benefit, over a period of time, the cost of living adjustment will increase that monthly benefit to keep up with inflation which will erode the buying power of the initial monthly benefit. Usually it's a certain percentage, say 3% of the monthly benefit. It could be compound or simple. While disabled, there's a waiver premium that kicks in. This means that while you're disabled after the elimination period - like any deductible - the waiver premium says you don't have to pay the premium. If and when you do recover and go back to work, all the back payments that are missed are wiped out. There are a few options which pay more if there's a catastrophic type of disability, which is similar to a long-term care where you have to be able to satisfy the two out of five ADLs (activities of daily living.)

Some carriers offer a return to premium option. For example, if somebody says that they will never use the policy because it's a waste of money, a nice rebuttal or another close would be, "Well, would you be happy if you would get all your money back, less paid claims, if you never use it?" It's a win-win situation.

DD: There's a lot of ability to customize the product based on the goals of the prospect and what they want to accomplish, like the length of the elimination period and benefit period. Are these some options that can be put into a disability product?

LS: Yes. There are also short and long benefit periods in addition to long and short elimination periods. This way, the product can be customized for someone who wants the policy but can't afford the premium. The two year benefit period brings down the premium dramatically. Later on, they can always trade in that policy for a longer term benefit period. When I say trade in, it'll be a reissue based on the age and new medical information. It's not literal trading where you get credit for the first one. You have to start all over again.

DD: One concern many new agents have is about the ideal prospects to target for disability insurance. Is there a particular group of people who make the best disability prospects? If so, who are they and how do you get in front of them? What is your preferred prospecting approach?

LS: That's a good question. First of all, most everyone is a prospect. There are also some prospects who are very difficult to approach. For example, a high income prospect like a doctor or an attorney. There will be many agents sitting in the waiting room the whole day to see this professional because everyone wants a high commission. My recommendation, especially for someone who is new, is to go to an area where very few agents have called on prospects so that you have a clear field. First of all, the person that you're speaking to is not yet sophisticated, or even aware on how a disability policy works. So you will be become their guru in terms of education, explaining everything about how it works.

As you develop knowledge, experience, learn to overcome objections, you go to the next level. I started off working in industrial centers making presentations to roofers etc, each working in a loft or a bay in an industrial center. Few agents go there. I was very successful and as I got more experience I was able to handle more objections with rebuttals and closing techniques. Thereafter, I went on to the next level of prospects like architects and psychologists. Psychologists work behind closed doors and agents don't know how to open those doors. In that case, along with everything else, you could do some direct mail - a letter that might get some interest.

These prospects will then call you and invite you to hear your presentation. As time passes by, you improve. Your level of expertise increases of course. You will be competitive in a niche market. In the beginning, I recommend new agents to stay away from a high commission prospect. They have been approached many times. Yet there's plenty of room. Disability insurance is an undersold commodity simply because most everybody is dealing with life insurance, health insurance, final expense, and so on. It's still a wide open market. There are plenty of opportunities with many published educational books on how to prospect, including mine.

DD: I used to have a fitness business and, one day, an insurance person walked in to talk about health insurance. He was the only insurance salesperson who walked in during those five years. The business people there, they are so head down into their business, plowing their profits and reinvesting, that they don't think about these policies. I imagine showing up is powerful, especially since there are less of us today than there used to be. I believe the business people are going to hear you out.

It sounds like you advocate a face-to-face approach at least initially rather than phoning for appointments.

LS: Absolutely. It's too easy for someone at the other end to say that they are busy and they will call back but they don't. There's no eye contact, no emotional connection. Instead, I would walk in on somebody and I would say, "I'm Larry Schneider and I have some very important information for you concerning the ownership of your business. Because this is confidential, I'll need a table where we can discuss it." It's a major type of hook that arouses curiosity - what are you talking about? What do you mean by the ownership of the business? 95% of the time I would be in their office 30 seconds later, doing my presentation. The truth is that a disability can cause loss of ownership of the business and is quite a powerful door opener.

DD: You said you have been in the business for 45 years, which means you started in disability in 1972. I'm sure that, like in many other lines of business, the insurance business has changed dramatically. I would like to know, what kind of changes have you seen? How have these changes affected the ability to sell and market insurance?

LS: It hasn't changed that much. You still have to create the need. The insurance industry has become more sophisticated in terms of underwriting. I would say that in the past things did slip by. But in today's market, the insurance underwriters have a lot of additional tools at their disposal to underwrite an application. I would say as a result, they probably put in a few more exclusions for pre-existing conditions than they did in the past. But at the same time, the product has become more liberal.

Nothing major has changed except enhancements and the issue/participation tables, which means how much can somebody get. For example, somebody who is making a million dollars a year is still going to get a capped to say $20,000. There's a point of diminishing returns. Someone making $50,000 a year will get roughly 60% of their income covered. Somebody who makes $100,000 will get $5,000 a month, whereas somebody who is making $200,000 is only going to get about $8,500. As the income goes up the issue chart allows less. The more you make, the lower the percentage becomes.

DD: What's the rationale behind that? Why do insurance carriers cap a lower percentage for the higher income earners?

LS: Well, that's a good question. You would think it would be a level playing field from that point of view. But the conservative powers to be ask how much anyone needs to pay their expenses. They want to give the claimant some motivation to quickly recover. If somebody is getting a straight 60% regardless of how much they are earning, they would think, "Why should I hurry up and recover? I'll sit on that boat for a couple of months." Granted that there has to be medical justification to being paid.

DD: We've been talking about the typical disability sale being to a white collar professional or a businessman and about the goal being to replace the income lost due to disability. What other type of financial solutions can disability insurance products be used for?

LS: In addition to getting an IDI - Individual Disability Insurance - there are other products that can be sold, such as a Business Overhead Policy (BOP), a separate policy to an IDI policy, which covers your income. A BOP pays the business expenses including a salary for somebody, rent, electricity, and so on. A BOP is a tax deductible premium, whereas the IDI premium is not. Even in cases where it is deductible, you shouldn't pay it with pre tax dollars because then the benefits are going to be taxable.

There is also a key man policy. Let's say you have a rainmaker working in the organization while the owner is playing golf. If that rainmaker goes down, the business is going to suffer. So, if you put a policy on that key man and if he or she become disabled, that money can go to the business where they continue to pay the key person, or hire somebody else and use that money to pay both their salaries. Another product is a buy sell policy. This is used to fund a partnership agreement. If one of the partners gets disabled, the able partner gets the money and will then pay the disabled partner to relinquish their share of the business. That's a very important product. In today's market, if I would go out selling again, I would focus on this type of policy because it makes you very unique in the marketplace.

The marketplace is not all that crowded. Few agents are selling disability insurance for various reasons. I would use a buy/sell presentation for a door opener in a partnership type of environment, whether attorneys or architects or

CPAs. In addition to having them as a client, they will give you a lot of referrals.

DD: Coming into this, when I train agents, what insurance they sell doesn't matter. I think it's extremely important to specialize and become master of one thing, at least initially. In the disability insurance market, is this something that you can solely sell and exclusively offer?

LS: Well, that's what I've done. The more you specialize, the more knowledgeable you become. It gives you credibility when you say, "I only sell disability insurance." You get some recognition from that statement since the client or the prospect believe that they are dealing with an experienced specialist. Your focus is on one product, so you had better know what you are talking about.

DD: What are the biggest advantages to the agent when selling disability insurance? Let's say we have an agent who is influenced by everything you've just said and is considering specializing in it. What are his advantages of selling that versus selling for example, life insurance to business owners?

LS: You are going to get an answer to that question by answering my question: Do you like working at night?

DD: No.

LS: Selling disability insurance is a daytime business. Plus, it has high commissions and persistency.

DD: That's a big deal. When we get into business, especially when we are younger, we don't mind working nights. For example, I've done 10+ years of grinding at 7pm, 8pm, 9pm, getting home by 10pm. Now my fourth kid is going to be here soon. We get to a point, even with ambition, where we want to retain some sort of family life and work during the day. It is a tremendous advantage.

LS: That's one part of it. Definitely, the commissions and the psychological income, i.e. knowing that you're going to be successful, are other additions to the total picture. Working daytime with high commissions and not having much competition (in life insurance everybody is grinding) are great advantages. I have worked nights, in the beginning, because a lot of my prospects were contractors and the blue collar market. They themselves were out working from nine to five. So much of my business came working from 5pm to 9 or 10pm. But to pay myself back then for not seeing my family, I only worked four days a week.

DD: *So you are not knocking doors, working nights. I think certainly there is some benefit in the long-term.*

LS: I also worked during the day but most of the business came at nighttime and was easy to sell to contractors because of the company's unique product. There was no deductible. Everybody got paid from day one. Everybody would be paid for their lifetime. So it was an easy product to sell. Plus, we had a presentation that was honed over many years. It took a half an hour to complete the presentation, but it was very convincing and had a lot of reverse psychology built into it. For example, we used phrases such as, "Let's see if you can qualify. I'll submit an application and see if it can be issued." Picture this; you go into a television store and you're negotiating with the salesperson. He says that this is the last one at a reduced price. Would that not be a magnet to make the sale? That is a little bit of reverse psychology.

Additionally, your persistency is going to be great because very few sales people are going to call on the same prospects. Even if you did, a couple of years have gone by where their health could have changed. You are going to have to overcome coverage for the new preexisting condition, which is not excluded in your client's current policy.

DD: *I'll add one thing. There's a point where if you're on a hamster wheel. You have to get up every morning and make a sale to make a living. You do that for 10 years, the renewals must be fantastic because this business so sticky. If you want to go down a couple of gears, you certainly can with the block of business that you've made.*

LS: Absolutely. In my business I am being reactive and not proactive. I get a lot of business through the Internet, through my reputation and through my articles and so on. I get business simply because of what I've done out there. There are the agents who call me - all the networking that I have done has now come to fruition.

DD: That's the advantage of being a specialist. Let's fast forward here. Imagine 20 years into the future. There's an awful lot of chatter and talk about how robots are going to take over the world and we're going to lose 75% of our jobs in 20 years. Where do you see disability sales and the insurance agent being in 20 years? Is the market going to be there? What are your thoughts on that?

LS: Disability insurance has been around for a hundred years. I don't see any major changes coming. As long as people are working and need an income, it will be around. The work force that may be going down because of robots is normally associated with a factory kind of environment. Disability insurance is not necessarily sold to a factory worker. The business owners are primary prospects. You can sell it to somebody who works in an office as an employee. They may already have coverage to a group long-term disability policy or have no coverage at all, incorrectly believing that the employee working for a company will be taken care of by the employer. I don't see the market changing in the next 20 years.

Robots are good when there is repetitive and redundant type of activity. They already have that in car manufacturing. For our market, for those who sell disability insurance, you'll not come face to face with a robot as your competition. I think there'll be plenty of opportunities and prospects. Sometimes there are not even enough hours in a day... if you want to pursue retiring sooner.

DD: That's a good idea. Just sell to the robot company owners. That's the solution.

LS: There you go!

DD: Larry, I've enjoyed this talk. If anybody is interested in talking to you directly, or in your books and material and training, how can they reach out to you?

LS: I have a toll free number which is 800-551-6211, cell 703-615-4747, or they can go to my website for some educational information. It's a consultative type of website where people can learn about disability insurance, gain confidence and get a good understanding of the ins and outs of disability insurance. They can also contact me.

My website is www.di-resource-center.com

E-mail: info@di-resource-center.com

DD: I would highly recommend purchasing the Encyclopedia of Disability book, which will make an agent an overnight expert. It does answer every question that you may have. Larry, thank you so much again for joining me today. I know people reading this will have found it extremely helpful.

LS: Thanks for allowing me to share. If anybody needs any insight or assistance they now know where to reach me. Best of luck to everybody.

How To Sell $280,000AP Of Final Expense Annually

Interview with Chris Grove

About Chris Grove

Chris is a final expense specialist selling since 2011. He has a very interesting story to tell, full of ups and downs. He's projecting that he will have issued around $280,000 business by the end of 2017, averaging about $5,500 in business produced weekly. As we get into this interview you're going to find that Chris has not always been successful selling insurance. This is why I'm glad to have him here today.

DD: Chris, tell us a little bit about yourself and how you've gotten here today.

CG: Sure. When I got out of high school I became a Marine. Then, when I left the Marine Corps, I became a nurse. Quite a transition! I guess it was a calling for me to have a job that for me, had purpose. The Marine Corps was for the country. My nursing was for seniors. But nursing wasn't for me. At 18 years old, one of my first jobs was telemarketing for the National Public Senatorial Committee. I would get people to donate money for a plaque or a calendar. I sold Kirby vacuums, Cutco knives, all of that stuff. It's built me up to where I am today.

Eventually I got into mortgages. I lucked out. I got in doing the refinance boom. I was one of these over-the-phone mortgage salesmen, improving my telemarketing resumé. It worked fantastically for me doing the refi boom until the market fell out. The way my business was set up, I didn't have affiliations to carry once the market crashed and they changed the business. So I left that and I went into auto sales. I did phenomenally well with auto sales, but it's one of the most negative industries you can work in. You work 80 hours a week for $60,000, $70,000 a year. It's not worth it.

Over the years I picked up different jobs serving in restaurants. At one time I was serving in a restaurant with a friend who worked three jobs. One of his jobs was assistant/secretary at Baltimore Life. He said to me that I should go in and check it out, that he thought it would be the right fit for me. And I went with them. I stayed there for a good year. I learned so many things. I learned the hard way, not the smart way, enough about the industry to discover that I wasn't doing what's best for my clients. The one-stop-shop is not best for everybody.

For me, morally, the second I found that out, I jumped ship. I had some recruiters that reached out to me, I guess that they ran across my policies. I reached back to one, landing in final expense.

DD: So you jumped right into a captive situation. These companies try to entice you in. We trust people by design until they prove otherwise. A lot of agents get started in the insurance business and they don't know anything. They simply don't. It's understandable.

Your experience was not great. You mentioned that it was a moral issue, which is an interesting way to put it. I feel the same way. You're brand new and getting into the captive environment. You're not going to think about this kind of thing. What kind of problems did you have in that type of environment? Why do you think it didn't sit so well with you?

CG: You've hit the nail on the head. Unless somebody knows your name and finds your videos on YouTube, they're not going to know. When you first go into something, you don't know. I try to explain this to my final expense clients all the time. If you don't know everything that's out there, you're not going to know that you're not doing what's best.

When I went with Baltimore Life, in my area, they were a great reputable company. I thought everything was well. It wasn't. I found out that there were other companies with much better pricing. Here's the best analogy. You can get a 12 pack of Charmin Ultra from Walmart for $15. You go to Target and it costs $20. Where should you be buying it from? The problem was that I was working for Target. It's the same product. For some products, sure, the reputation of the company, their assets, and their ratings can be important. But for certain things, no. In final expense, it doesn't matter, unless you have a company that doesn't pay claims.

So, that was the main reason for me leaving. There were other things. I'm the kind of person who is not meant to have a boss. I'm not meant to answer to anybody. I was not built to be an employee. Working for Baltimore Life, there were three meetings a week. You had to show up every morning at 8:00 am, in your tie and jacket. One of the things we did was to go to the courthouse and take the newly recorded deeds. We would take the names and addresses and bring them back to the office. We'd type up the letter, mail the letter and try to solicit term life insurance coverage.

Friday was my day to do that. And every Friday my manager and I would have an argument. He expected me to show up at the office in a suit and tie first. That way, he knew that I was in a suit and tie before I went to the courthouse. The problem was that the office was on the other side of town, and the courthouse was in between the office and my home. I said, "Look, man, you don't cut me a check. I'm a commissioned employee, this isn't flying."

It wasn't a good fit. It wasn't working. It didn't work with my personality. I didn't like the office environment, the way things were. But the main thing that I didn't like was working harder, not smarter. But then again, I guess I realize that more now than I did then.

As far as the clients go, I was not a big fan of fully underwritten. You wait 30 to 45 days, things go south, you're waiting for APS and Parameds. It was also the clients that you sit in front of. Unless you truly learn how to network market, getting a BNI type deal, even if you're doing term, the average client that you sit in front of would say, "Oh, I've got insurance with work" or "I've got that term" or "I'm in my thirties, I'm good on this."

To be successful in a fully underwritten world, you have to build that base up to where you're dealing with the higher level of clientele. A clientele that needs the coverage more than someone who is good with what they have from work. There is still more of a need, but for somebody with 2.5 kids, a brand new mortgage, and car payments, I have to cover all those bills. There's only so much income to go around.

To me, that goes with the same level of working harder, with the idea of sitting in a BNI group and doing all this network marketing. That's not me either. That's not how I'm built. I don't kiss anybody's butt. I'm not the golf course guy. I'm not the guy hanging out with you at the bar every Wednesday to pick up your referrals. That's not who I am.

So it wasn't the best fit for me. My true talent shows when I'm sitting in front of someone. It's not doing all that other back-end stuff. It's being in front of them doing my thing. Doing my years of telemarketing, Kirby, auto sales, and mortgage sales. Moving my mouth. That's where my success is. I've always looked at it as, if I'm not sitting in front of a person selling to them, it's my time wasted. The idea of doing all this other harder work to get to that point didn't seem very efficient for my style or for what I'm best suited to.

DD: I'm the same way. I've always had an anathema, some sort of resistance to asking for people to refer me business. It's not that it doesn't work. It's that it's always been like a wall to climb over with the whole BNI thing. I know exactly what you mean. I want to see people that are at least a little bit interested and I want to see a lot of them.

There are a couple of things you brought up that I thought were pretty interesting. Chris, you have transitioned from captive non final expense to independent final expense. I'm just like you, I believe the best way to be in final expense, if not all insurance sales, is to be independent. You have more options to give your clients. You get them a better deal. You're less biased than you are if you push one product. Do you think that all agents can succeed independently? Do some of them require the trappings of captivity, like having a boss and being micromanaged? Is every agent cut out to be independent?

CG: If you need that captivity, it doesn't make you a bad agent. Some people need hand-holding and coddling, they need support. But if you need that, you're not meant for this industry. It's not the best fit for you. A good agent in this industry can be independent. Guys that are with Baltimore Life now try to replace my policies. I'll have a conversation with them. The conversation turns into a heart to heart. Now, I don't recruit. So it's not hard to say to them, "Why are you doing it? Here's the reason why I left the company you're working for. Why are you doing it? You're not doing what's best for the people in front of you. Your bias is that you're selling that company. Your obligation is to the company rather than to the person in front of you."

The greatest statement that I can say to my clients now is that I have their best interests at heart. I don't cater to any company's interests. If I don't want to talk to a company right now, I don't talk to them. I do what's best for the client. That's the way it should be in any industry. If you're working for a captive company, you're wrong. That's my opinion. You should always do what's best for the people in front of you. Never do what's best for an organization. One of the big reasons why our industry has so many failures is because agents get stuck in the mindset that they do need captivity.

I was talking to one guy, he said, "Well, I've got some medical issues and they have a great health care package."

"My income doubles or triples yours," I told him, as humbly as possible. "You could pay for your own healthcare."

Thinking that you need this comfort, needing to rely on somebody else to take care of you, that's not a mindset that can succeed in independent final expense. You've got to be an entrepreneur. I'm an entrepreneur. That's who I am. If you don't have that mindset and drive, you're not going to make it in final expense.

DD: You need to be looking at this business as an actual career, not as a short-term flash in the pan project. As with any insurance agent on straight commission, we wake up every morning not knowing if it could be our last day. Of course, it won't be if you follow the system. But, to have that level of commitment and long-term success requires something more than a typical employee mentality. That's the essence of what a captive company provides. They sell the idea of independence, you have your own business, you work when you want. You really don't. Look at the captive environment. They force you into the meetings. You answer to somebody. You are an employee rather than having your own business as an agent. Nobody cares about you. You're on your own. That's hard on people who do it on a long-term basis.

CG: Like I said, every Friday this 'manager' would call me up and say, "Why aren't you here?" He treated me like an employee. It's how it works. I had to have the argument with him. Finally, it got to the point where I started ignoring his calls. It wasn't going to happen. It's never going to happen. I'm not coming in to make him feel warm and fuzzy because I'm wearing a suit and tie. I'm there at the courthouse, I'm doing my thing and I'm in shorts and flip-flops, deal with it.

DD: How did you get out of being captive and into final expense? What attracted you to final expense?

CG: A couple of series of events started the transition. The first series was that they hired a new employee (because that's what you are, an employee) in my office at Baltimore Life. He had come from Lincoln Heritage and he needed the hand holding. That's why he left Lincoln Heritage. In conversations with him, he would tell me about working there.

I actually started talking to them. Thank God that never proceeded any further, but while he was in the office I was already starting to look for my window out.

Then our regional manager decided to purchase NetQuote leads. NetQuote doesn't pay attention to the fact that there are people buying from under the same umbrella company. I was purchasing leads and they were selling leads to my co-worker. We ended up getting the exact same leads. I brought that to the attention of Baltimore Life. I said, "Look, I'm buying leads to write business for your company and you're supplying those leads to my competition, who is also my co-worker!"

"It just is what it is," they said.

And that was the door opening. I immediately started working my way out.

The other series of events started when I was recruited. A couple of different people had a couple of recruiters reach out to me. I guess they ran into my policies, that's how they found me. I stored their numbers on my phone, or on a piece of paper somewhere. When they first reached out to me I did feel that I needed that company. I felt that I needed that level of support because I didn't know the industry. I was so green. So at first, I ignored these recruiters. Once I had that mindset of knowing that I had to get out and find something else to work, I reached out. I broke those numbers out and talked to them and we had more in-depth conversations. I ended up getting going with an organization based out of Maryland. They were a final expense operation. They did nothing but Columbian Life, Transamerica, which was called Monumental at the time, and Kemper. That was it. That was their portfolio. Having a portfolio so restricted would be enough for me to transition out of them. The main reason, however, was that I knew that I was being sold leads that were resold and stomped all over. Things weren't working there. That was the transition.

DD: How was your first year or two in the business as you have got into the position you're now in? Did you have success? Did you have failures? How would you describe it?

CG: I failed miserably. I failed for a solid two, two and a half years. I don't know why I'm here today. I did believe in it because I did have some mini successes. What I mean by mini success is that I did have those big sales. I went out and I had sales that paid me over $1000 at my ridiculously low commission levels of the time. I saw the sales come in and I saw it even with the resold leads, doing nothing but door knocking. We couldn't call first. We were told not to because the company knew they were people that had been already called. We were getting the leftovers.

I still saw how easy it could be. You could walk into somebody's home, you've never met them before and from a cold door knock, you could walk out an hour later with $1000. I believed that there had to be some way to get that to repeat more often. I made enough money to get by at times. I had faith that something was there. I could not believe that it was me that was failing. It had to be something else there that was failing. Everyone in my family said, "Are you sure this is for you?" My mother, my grandparents, "Are you sure it's for you?" They saw the failures. Man, are they all eating their words now!

DD: They can't understand why we do this. Did anybody try to talk you out of it?

CG: My grandfather. He sold insurance years ago. I can't even remember the name of the company that he worked for. He did door to door monthly to pick up the premiums. For the first couple of years that I was doing it, he talked about how hard it was and how he failed out of it. He was convinced that I was going to fail out of it. Now, over the last three years, I've been told how proud everyone is of me. How amazed they are at the change. They can't believe that it turned from what it was to what it is now.

I failed to the point that the brokerage that I was with was not working. I was trying to look at another brokerage and we were making the transition. There were issues with them getting me leads. At that point, I had to pick up a side job working with a construction crew. 80% of the people on the crew were in a halfway house or were drug addicts. This was an under the table job. I was getting up at 6:00 am, getting back at 5:00 pm, driving two hours to Virginia. We were doing an apartment complex with five stories. When you're five stories up, you're supposed to have harnesses and safety equipment. We were doing the gutter, I'm hanging half of my body off of this building. I'm looking down to the ground thinking, "There's my death. Right there. That's it. That's my death."

You're freezing, you're outside and you're hanging off this thing. If you slip the wrong way you're done for. This guy hadn't given us the harnesses that we needed. About 20 minutes later we were on lunch break and I called up the guy that was recruiting me. I said, "Dude, you need to get me leads tomorrow. I needed them yesterday. I'm not built for that. I need them now."

That's the level of failure I was at. I failed to where I took up that kind of under the table construction work with co-workers in halfway houses. But I still had faith that something was there. Something told me to continue. That IMO didn't work but I eventually transitioned to the right one.

DD: I hope you new guys are listening to this. Those thinking about getting started in some sort of insurance. Or even if you're experienced and you're going through hard times. This is an important thread that I try to hit on with all my interviews. It's the one consistent factor between all the successes that I have spoken to. If there were failures, they didn't quit. They had every reason to quit. Their family told them to. Their loved ones told them to. Under any rational circumstance all the signs pointed to quitting, but for whatever reason they continued to have faith. Some people were religious about it. I went through the same thing you did, Chris. You've seen my videos. Everything you're saying, I agree with. The similarities between the guys that do well in selling insurance are amazing. They all have a failure story. For whatever reason, pigheaded discipline, determination, they kept on and on. Sometimes that's what it comes down to. That's the difference.

Let's talk about your transition from failure to success. What was the turning point? What brought you to your current level of production?

CG: I was recruited by YIG, Your Insurance Group, through an agent who had run across some of our policies. He was very familiar with the organization that I was working with, which was a split off from Securus. When it fell apart half of the agents went to YIG and the rest went to the Willis Agency down in Maryland and Virginia. I was with the Willis Agency and this YIG guy who recruited me said, "Look, they don't know what to do. We have better carriers. You need to come with us."

When they brought me over, the big change was in the leads. For the first time in two and a half years, I was not working leads that were already worked. And that was it. My very first week door knocking with leads that were never previously worked, I pulled $7,300AP. The very first week. That was from taking two to three months to make $7,300AP. That's why I'm saying that I was failing. I would make that $1000 sale, but it was once every two or three weeks. But I had known that there was a way to repeat it. I went from that to $7,300 a week door knocking. That was it. It was finally having the correct lead source that put me in front of people, gave me a reason to be in their doorway.

Not one of them said, "Look, somebody has already been here last week!" Of course, you can get that anyway in the industry. But if somebody was there last week it wasn't because they were using the exact same leads. No one was saying, "We told him over the phone not to come! Why are you here?" I didn't have that as much. It had toned down. They got to see the lead, they got to see that it was their handwriting, see it in my name. It was fresh. It was something that was recently done.

Here's the faith part of it. How hard it was to make the decision to be put on a recurring lead order. To say, "Here's my money, here's $500 (it was only 20 leads). I'm going to give you $500 next week and I'm going to give you $500 the week after that. I did not have that $500, let alone the $1000 or $1500. I did not have it. It was credit cards that paid for that. How hard to make that decision and put in that order through email. When I put it in I sat there and prayed as I hit the enter button. I'll never forget that day that I prayed before I hit that button. It took a lot to hit it because once I hit it that morning, that was it.

The main part was those leads. I had my natural talents and I had the years of sales. I knew I could do it. I found the right scripts, the right process. The final thing that made the switch was having the right leads.

DD: *Are you saying that the biggest determinant here, going from mediocrity to top 5%, was a simple shift in leads? You did it because you went from working aged, resold leads to exclusive fresh leads?*

CG: It made at least 80% of the difference.

DD: *There are agents out there that are right now going through the same thing that you went through. If they only knew that they could get leads that weren't resold and that were fresh. Do you think that could change their lives as well?*

CG: No. It's the mentality as well. I'm part of a chat group. One of the biggest agents in the country and the industry has let me be a part of his chat group, which I'm very grateful for. In the chat group, I bite my tongue because it's his. I don't say things that are out of my place. This week, one of his agents put a post up saying, "Where are the $6 leads?"

I wanted to jump on and ask him, "Dude, what are you doing?" I didn't, because it's not my place. It's not my chat. I'm just allowed to be in it.

You can't sit there and think that $6 per lead is going to get you anywhere. Those are fillers. You'll be broke, living in your mommy's basement, having to buy with credit cards. You have to believe in yourself. You have to take that leap. You can't do this career going the cheap way. Have I made money off aged leads? Sure. I've sold to leads that were two years old. They're there, but they're not what's going to keep you writing $7,300 a week. You're not writing $7,300 a week, or even $5000, or even $4000. You're not writing that consistently off of aged leads.

You need fresh leads. You need to be in front of somebody. To me, it's a combination of everything. It's your script, it's your way of going about it. Putting yourself in front of somebody. Your comfort level of being in someone's home and getting in the door. The pitch that you use. And having best carriers, you need that too. Without them, there are so many houses where you would not have got the replacement. You would not have been able to write that person. They would have thought, "Two years?" and they would have thrown their hands in the air. Two years, where if you have the right carrier, they would have got day one coverage. You would have never had that to overcome. All these other parts are important to me.

The number one thing, in the beginning, is the marketing. Working smarter, not harder. The smartest way to do this business is to spend $30,000, $40,000 a year throwing leads at it. BNI group? Going to the courthouse for mortgage leads? Working referrals, working this, working all that? No. You make a credit card payment, leads show up every single week. That gives you 20, 25, 30 opportunities to sit in front of somebody every week that nobody else has sat in front of. You can hand the lead to them. They see their handwriting and they see their name assigned to you at the top. That is the most important of the big group of things that will make you successful.

DD: Like you said, you need the right mentor, the right training, and the right leads. That is the critical aspect that a lot of people don't understand. They think that they can be cheap about it. They think, "I'll take the cheaper leads. I'll still do okay." It never works out that way.

CG: Especially in the beginning when you have competition, replacements. People are going to fall off anyway because they made the emotional decision, then they regret it. When you put all that in the mixture, and then add chargebacks, you need the right leads. That's the whole thing.

You buy one set of leads and sell whatever you get off of that. Then you decide to buy another set of leads. It's leads, and then it's recurring. It's the two of them combined. It's a recipe for failure. Telemarketing leads? Sure, I've got sales from them. But I can't stand those leads for two reasons. First of all, it's definitely 100% lower level. The other part is that you have to work a much larger area. These telemarketing lead companies need a lot of data.

Direct mail is the easiest lead for them to get larger percentages in a confined space. That puts you in front of more people. You're starting out in the industry and you're traveling three hours from appointment to appointment. You will only have three appointments a day with telemarketing leads instead of six, seven, or eight with direct mail. You can't be spread out everywhere and make it efficient. In the beginning, you have to work in a smaller space. That way you can get to all these homes, especially if you're door knocking and no one is home.

I mark that house where they're not home to try again. Say I tried it at 11:00 am, I'll try them again at 4:00 pm. They're still not there, I'll try again at 6:00 pm. If every house is two hours away from any others, that is so inefficient. It's not going to work. As a filler after, it would be a great resource. You get your 20 direct mail leads every week, then put those in to fill in those gaps to get those appointments for Wednesday, Thursday, Friday if you work it. They're great for that, but they're not the bread and butter leads.

My mind has, however, been changed on Facebook leads. These are on a level where they're separating themselves from telemarketing leads and other leads. I've actually been using them, purchasing them consistently since April. My setter says that they set easier and my sales are higher compared to direct leads. You get the same stuff, of course, the same crap, people think that it's going to be free, all that. They even have a slightly higher percentage of sales for me than direct leads, but the problem with them is the same as telemarketing leads. You can only get so much in that area. They still have that data issue. The right way to take them is to learn how to perfect them in a way that they can be great. I still don't know if I would ever suggest starting my career with them. You need to be an experienced agent before you jump in with them.

To start your success, it's direct mail leads. If you talk to the big organizations that are out there, they all do it a certain way. If any of these other organizations try to sell you a better way, say, "No." These ones are proven. They are used for a reason. There are hundreds, thousands of agents that are successful in this industry and they all start with direct mail that's fresh, not aged. If you believe in yourself then take that leap and spend that money. If you don't believe in yourself, don't even do the aged leads. Don't waste your money.

If you believe in yourself, then why don't you spend the money to do the same thing everybody else does? Maybe you believe in yourself so much that you think that you don't need to spend $30 a lead because you can do it off the $6 lead. All the successful agents, we need the $30 lead. If you think that you're so much better than us, nothing is going to work out for you.

I will say that I do my own script. I don't know any other agencies that teach my approach in the house. I don't do what everybody else does. I also have my setter doing things differently when setting the appointment. My appointments have no clue that it's about life insurance. That's never mentioned. Her job is to get me to a home. That's it. To me that increases my numbers. It puts me in front of more people. At the end of the day they filled the lead out. They should know that it's about insurance. To me it makes no sense, if you have insurance already with Lincoln Heritage or whoever and somebody calls you up and tells you that their guy is going to come over and they mention life insurance. You're going to ask, "Why? I've got insurance!" There goes your chance to be in front of the house for replacement. So I do those things differently to how I understand the rest of the industry does.

At the same time, it's still pretty much the same system. You buy direct mail leads. You get in front of people. You do a pitch. It may not be the same one that the majority of the industry uses, but it's still a pitch that makes sense, it still finds the reasons, the right way. It's a system that starts with direct mail.

One year I was taking a trip. On the way down I listened to your videos, David. All the videos, all the way there and back. My entire trip. It was three hours out and three hours back, six hours of nothing but me and David Duford. Afterward, I reached out to you saying, "Why did I not find you three years ago? Why did I not? Everything that was said in them I learned, but I learned the hard way. If I had spent six hours then watching your videos, man, it would have saved me so much time, struggle, frustration! I probably wouldn't have failed out in the industry. I would have learned those things then, that it took all this time to learn."

DD: Thanks! Continuing on, a lot of guys know who you are. You talk with a lot of different agents, some successful, some not successful. Based on your interactions with other final expense agents, why do you think some of these agents succeed and others fail?

CG: A lot fail because they're with a crap IMO. There's a lot of bad marketing organizations out there. There's a lot of bad brokerages. And their commission levels! That's the whole thing, there is a lot of expense. To be successful in this industry, you need direct mail leads. Direct mail leads cost a lot of money. You're not going to write that much business, especially in the beginning. There's going to be a learning curve as you gain experience. You're not going to do $4000, $5000, $6000, $7000, or $8000 weeks. You're definitely not going to do it every single week. You need proper contract levels. There's a lot of money that you're putting out in your business, with the gas, going out there, everything else that's involved. To have chargebacks coming off that money, you need to have enough there. To have enough there, you need the correct contract levels. There's a lot of marketing organizations that give these ridiculous levels. They're taking way too much profit from your work. Whether they train you or not, there's a certain level that's too low. That adds to the recipe for failure. You're spending $600 a week on leads and you're writing $2000 a week. That's awesome. But if your commission levels are low and after all your expected expenses, you're only getting $600 or $700 a week income, is this career worth it? 60 to 70 hours a week of dealing with all the crap we deal with and the type of clientele we deal with for $600 or $700? It's not worth it. That's where it's so easy to say, "No, I'm out this insanity. I need to go home and be with my family. This is not worth it." It's the bad IMO.

David, you bring this up all the time; making sure you know your contracts, if you're vested, and if you have open releases and things like that which are extremely important. You give a service to the industry, apart from recruiting. The big impressive thing about your videos is that whether you recruit or not, you help agents. If an agent comes across your video, whether you gain anything from it or not, they at least have been told. They know what to look for now. Going with the crap IMO gets you the crap leads that they supply.

My first organization, Willis Agency, was a recipe for failure. I had low contracts and I had leads that were resold. There was no way for me to be successful in that environment. As I look back, I don't see how that makes any sense. If you want to recruit an agent, why would you not want them to be successful? Why would you not give them the tools to be successful?

That's a big part of it. Then, multiple carriers. You need multiple carriers because that opens more sale opportunities for you. You're sitting in a house. They have COPD and they already have a graded policy. You don't have a Transamerica or Liberty Bankers or Equity policy, something that can get them day one coverage. Yes, your cover may be cheaper than the crap graded policy that's costing them $80 a month. You might be able to save them $30 a month, but you can't light it legally. You need those other tools to be able to pick up those sales. It gives you more opportunity.

Another thing is being aggressive. I am very aggressive. I call my sales pitch, "No sales". When I sit with a client, I educate them. I give them a life insurance 101. I explain it to them so they understand it. The what, the when, the why. Why they should do this one, when they need to do it. How the costs are set. Why I'm choosing this company, why it's the best fit for them. How the industry works. I guide them in that way. I'll even show them. I'm giving them the best company that fits for them. The best that they qualify for. Instead of selling them something, I explain it to them. I educate them so they finally understand. To me, 90% of the products and services we have, we were sold. We weren't told, we weren't educated.

That's a big part of it. Even the AP clients can read a slimeball. They can read the car salesman. If you come into this industry to be a salesman, you're going to fail a lot. You'll get enough, but you won't be able to get as much as you could have doing it my way. For me, it goes back to faith. I will always be honest and do what's best for the person in front of me. Don't ever do what's best for your company. Don't ever do what's best for yourself. Do what's best for the person in front of you. Whether you want to call that Karma or God thanking you for doing it that way, that's a huge part of your success as well.

If you go in as a salesman, you do what's best for yourself. I know that there are guys out there that this works for, but it would work better if you did what's best for the people in front of you. You will get those referrals down the road. A lot of people say that in this industry, nobody picks up the phone and calls you. Well, after years in this industry, people call me. Not too often, but I get referral calls. They tell me that I signed them up two or so years ago. They've since had three or four agents come in the house and none of them could touch their policy. They say, "The agents all get pissed off when they see what you gave me and they can't touch it. They can't do anything about it! It finally made me realize that you did such a great job for me. So I'm telling everybody I know about you!"

If you don't do it for the person in front of you, you're not going to have that experience. You write them these higher, more expensive carriers because they give you the best permission rate, you'll get replaced. Not only do you lose your business, but you lost any chance of ever getting a referral from them either.

DD: How many agents in this business have failed out because they're honest? Sometimes they fail out because they're dishonest. Something comes back to them and causes them harm. What if you just do the right job? Yes, you may not make as many sales, but it's a short-term sacrifice which is in truth, not a sacrifice. It's a long-term investment in your career. It creates good karma like you've said. It's investing in the longer term.

CG: I write the cheapest carriers and I do that to increase retention. I believe God will provide and he has provided for me very well. They say that it's quality that matters, not quantity. Well, quality has become quantity. It has. I don't need to write those higher commission carriers because I do have enough coming in. It's all going to be fine. Doing that gives me the retention for future renewals. If people do find out, nobody can beat the price. No other agent can come in and replace you. And it's not only the income that you make now, it's the income you make for the next five to six to seven years. Then the same thing recurring from your renewals. The better you do for the person in front of you, the better that chance gets also.

It seems so easy to me. There are so many times when I walk into a house and zone out completely and my entire pitch comes out. It's memorized at this point. Much as an actor does, I zone out. I will be on my phone, looking at Facebook, and I'll sell my entire pitch. I've done it. That's how easy it is. It's the other things that make me that success. The problems are these carriers not being aggressive, not doing what's best, the bad leads. But it also comes down to the fact that some people have it, some don't.

DD: Final expense is unique relative to other businesses. There's this big push to be aware of things like social media, technology, and how it impacts our ability to sell. When it comes to selling to Millennials, they don't want to be sold. They want to do everything online. Whereas, in final expense, we've been doing the same thing with direct mail for 30 years or longer. You have experience in dealing with these people on a daily basis. Where do you see final expense as a business model in the next 20 years? What kind of changes, if any, do you suppose will happen with how we prospect for business, the kind of people that we see?

CG: It will be the exact same way it is now. I've thought about this a lot. Technology is a big part of the world we live in, there is absolute truth to that, but at the same time, the Millennials are not our clients now. They might be our clients 20 years from now, but I still believe that it's not going to change and here's the reason why. It's not politically correct, but it's simple fact. Our clients did not do life right.

You're sitting in front of me at 60, 65, 70 years old and you're living paycheck to paycheck. You're renting and you have all these co-pays on your meds. This is the other reality. If you're in that situation, you've probably lived the life of drugs, alcohol, and abuse. Job to job, paycheck to paycheck, you don't have retirement and a pension. You did not do life right. I can't be politically correct about this. What those years of that lifestyle that you lived did was to dumb you down. All that affects you mentally and you dumb yourself down to where you need that hand holding.

Our clients need that coddling, that trust. They feel that everyone has taken advantage of them their entire life. That's why they're in the situation they're in. They need someone to come in so that they can see that trust in them. If you're a salesy person, they're going to see that and it's not going to work. They'll think that they are getting taken advantage of yet again. They need to see someone that they can trust.

They're not going to trust the Internet. My mom refuses to have Facebook. She refuses to have anything out there on the internet because she's 100% positive that people want to break into her home. They will steal all her stuff, her bank account. The Internet is the devil. That attitude will continue. These people are our clients. I hear the story all the time where somebody calls them up from a different country. They speak very little English. They tell them that they're having computer issues and they need to get into their computer, into their bank account. And the clients allow it! You're not the sharpest tool in the shed to have that happen to you, are you? That's the reality.

My calling is to save those people. I could take advantage of them. I could go in their home and I could take advantage of them for my own financial gain. I'm smart enough and I'm savvy enough that I could, but I refuse to. That's where my calling is. To put more money on the table for food. More money on the table for medications. Giving them the best coverage, explaining it to them, and doing everything to prevent them from being taken advantage of any more.

They will always meet us. They will always want that face to face interaction. If you are good at what you do, you get your butt to that couch or that dining room table and all you need to do with the opportunity is to say, "Well, your telephone sales guy sounded awesome. He gave you this great Foresters or Royal Neighbours phone sales pitch." I've got nothing against those companies. They're great, but if all that they have is phones sales and I have Family Benefit or Mutual or KSKJ in my bag, now I'm replacing that policy. I don't care how it was over the phone, how great it sounded. At the end of the day, you're on a budget and if I save you $10, $15, $20 a month, how many meals is that? They're going to do it.

I don't think we're going to have that much of a change for our clients. The rest of the world? Absolutely. From final expense and Medicare to the

Medicaid Advantage type clients, they will always write us. The rest of the world, they're all going to change.

DD: If I may quote scripture here, Ecclesiastes says that there's nothing new under the sun. You may change the medium in which people request information. We may do more Facebook and internet stuff 20 years from now. I wouldn't be surprised. But the nature of people will pretty much stay the same. There will be people who have avoided the responsibility of life insurance and owning it for so long. Now they're sick and they've had a brush with death or they've lost a loved one. They're experiencing the same thing as our people are today. They're going to have the same fears. We're all pretty much the same. We experience the same fears and apprehensions. A lot of agents in traditional life markets don't understand that the final expense mentality is completely different. These agents, it's hard to describe it to them. It's a huge market, but most people don't have first-hand experience with the differences.

Chris, I want to express my gratitude and appreciation for a great interview. I really enjoyed this and my audience will love and appreciate what you have to say. We covered a lot of different topics on final expense. I appreciate your time and thank you so much for taking time out of your day to do this.

CG: My pleasure. Let's take a moment to actually have a little bit of a prayer here.

Lord, I wanted to thank You for the opportunity and the blessing that You've given me. I'm amazed by Your grace. By where I am, the accomplishments that I've been able to achieve in life because of You. I want You to help out anybody listening to this. Please, Lord, if there's anybody hearing this that You can help, give Your assistance and guidance to make it in this career. If this career is not meant for them, please, as politely as possible, show them the doors as soon as possible so they don't waste their time. Help them to be able to provide for their family.

In Jesus' name, we pray. Amen.

Interview With Nick Williams, The Medicare Millionaire

About Nick Williams

Nick has been in the insurance and financial services business, building agencies and agents for 30 years. He is the owner of Medicare Millionaire, where he trains agents how to sell Medicare Supplements face to face.

DD: Nick Williams, welcome to the show.

NW: Hello Dave. Glad to be here.

DD: Thanks for coming on. I want to start off with your YouTube channel first. Can you describe what you do and who you're trying to target in your insurance YouTube channel?

NW: Well, my YouTube channel is a result of my failure. I've had great successes and then I got into lull, and for several years I was sliding. I came across internet marketing. I found it to be very exciting and that lit the fire. I married internet marketing with my insurance business and started getting getting back on track. I started making daily videos explaining what I was doing on a that specific day and sharing some knowledge. I stayed with it and really enjoy it. It's growing into more than a daily video.

DD: I think what's unique about your channel is that it is a personal, honest interaction on a day to day basis with an insurance agent in the trenches, which is more valuable than flash and materialistic objects. So people actually get to learn something.

NW: One thing I'll add here is that 90 percent of the agents fail in the first year. I could be wrong, but certainly the 80-20 rule applies. It's a shame, isn't it? I mean that people come into any business with hopes and dreams. It's a big deal. But then it all falls apart. So wouldn't it be nice to do something for those people, Dave? That's really what this is about.

DD: I can tell you the one thing about this profession in general is that it's a very lonely one. Most of us who are out there are on our own. We get up, have to motivate ourselves out the door and meet people, set appointments, and deal with rejection. This job is very hard for somebody who's not in sales. I understand it is all up in your head. It's an emotional roller coaster. The great thing about your channel is you get to see both good and bad days, which is very helpful for the person who is getting started or frustrated. It helps a lot to have someone to share that with and understand you're not alone out there.

NW: Yes. There are a many of us. I saw a statistic where there are 300,000 licensed health agents.

DD: Can you tell us about your background and how you got involved in the insurance?

NW: Interestingly enough, it was an AL Williams Rah Rah meeting, which is now a Primerica. I never did sign up with AL Williams. I went to a meeting one day and they were all chanting 'Boca, Boca', and it seemed a little scary. They were out for a trip Boca Rotan. This was when I lived in Maryland. A friend of mine had a Midland National Life Insurance Agency. It was a little hole-in-the-wall agency. I went in there and I cranked it out.

Prior to that, I was a military person, so I did the military thing. Then I was a union person and I was never comfortable with it. I saw the insurance business as my ticket and I chased it. There were ups and downs along the way. But here I am 30 years later.

DD: It seems that the main focus on your channel is Medicare Supplements. So what I would like to hear more about is the reason you sell Medicare Supplements at this point in your career? Why did you choose that per se as your focus versus other products?

NW: I've done the seminar circuit. I call it big game hunting. I used to do three seminars every month for annuities. You live by the sword, die by the sword. I did one thing that had saved me - I had medicare renewals coming in and it's common sense that the renewals are fairly substantial if you get a good number of medicare supplements and medicare advantage clients on the books. While it wasn't enough to carry me, it saved me from falling. Then I realized this is what I've got to build up. I also sell final expense, the indemnity products, and I'll grab the annuity but I don't chase annuities. It's about the renewals. It's about waking up and already having a check without having to sell anything. That's my logic.

DD: Yes. I can tell you from personal experience, and obviously I tell agents that the biggest weakness of final expense is that their renewal is not much. While I think it's a great place to start since you get more experience in the business or get older, you start to get passive income or renewal income.

NW: Yes. Renewals, the persistency of the medicare business is extremely good. Even when I haven't been attentive to my book of business, I've maintained a fair amount of clientele.

DD: Like you said, life changes and you may not want to work as much at some point. You might want to slow down. So I think it's smart to have that as a piece of your business. So, let's talk about what top producers have to say about how they run their business. What I'm curious to hear, Nick, is a breakdown of your typical week in the field - from setting appointments, running appointments, servicing clients. How do you do your week?

NW: Well, I have a telemarketer working 40 hours a week. I work very closely with her. I have salesdialers.com working and it's a very smooth system. Every day I'm booked so I have more leads than I can ever work. On average, I have about 10 new leads every day. You probably know if you get out there and start selling, you're not going to make it to 10 houses, but even if you might make it to 10 in one day, you could get nothing. I do that. So I'll get up, pack a cooler with six to eight water bottles in ice and I'm on the road.

I check to make sure I got my bag together and clipboard with all the appointments listed. So when I get to the door, I'm official. I approach and say "You talked to Rachel in my office yesterday about the Medicare. I'm here to see if I can help you out". I show them the clipboard and they get interested. So now I'm in the grind. That's what it's all about. Getting out the door and grinding. The same thing can be done on the phone, except you don't have to pack a cooler. Selling over the phone is also a grind in one way or the other. That's the way I look at it.

DD: Well you need a track to run on, right? You've got a system you have to implement, and that's what it's all about - constant daily implementation. Let me ask a question - it sounds like you don't really set any of your appointments. Your appointment setter does all that work for you. Correct?

NW: Yes. I think that's smart. My appointments are set for A.M. or P.M. I don't set exact times. I figure seniors are going to be home. You set five appointments in a day which might be when people aren't home. So I show up and if I don't get to the lead on that day, I'll get there the next day, put up a big smile on my face, and say that I was supposed to be here the previous day but I got tied up. They let you in and you do your thing. That's my approach.

DD: So when your appointment setters sets a call they ask 'when do you want Nick to show up? In the morning or afternoon? What works better?'

NW: Yes. It's 'morning or afternoon' and 'it's a very simple presentation' or 'we would help you with your medicare supplement insurance' or 'we are going to have somebody in your area tomorrow to go over any changes that may occur that would affect you either positively or negatively'. The prospects might give a rebuttal saying they already have an agent to which we say 'Well that's fine. We want to go over the changes in medicare and determine if there's any help that we can provide you. Would morning or afternoon be better?' Then we let them go. We don't push for an appointment.

DD: What are your daily appointment goals and how many days a week do you run in field?

NW: I have 10 leads every day - that's what I average. I very seldom make it to 10 houses. Sometimes I go to more than 10. I mapped them out with Microsoft Streets and Trips for the most efficient route and I'll run them. So, my goal is to sell every day, which I usually do. If I make one sale every day, I'm very happy. I've got to the point where I am a little bit disappointed that I only have one sale a day.

DD: Absolutely. So when you say you've got 10 fresh leads that come in on an average daily basis, you're seeing them the next day. Is that correct? Maybe some days you miss and see them on the other days. is that your approach?

NW: Yes, What I do is I incorporate the new leads into the ones that I didn't see and then I reroute them on Microsoft Streets and Trips.

DD: So you don't work evenings? So you're home by dinner time every night then?

NW: Yes. Unless I choose to work late. You probably realize that when you have a YouTube channel or similar platforms, it can take up a lot of time. So I have to make decisions about when I'm working. I consolidate my sales to blocks and so consider it more of a blitz. I don't find it necessary to work into the evening often.

DD: Sure. Do you ever flat out door knock leads? It sounds like you have people you miss, but do you ever show up unannounced without ever having called to attempt for an appointment?

NW: No. I have too many leads for that. I make it easy on my telemarketer to get me a lot of appointments. I give a simple telemarketing script - I don't want to know about health or the plan they have or any qualifying questions. Several weeks ago, she got me 19 in one day. I get there and then it's about the agent. When agents are not selling they get frustrated that these leads are useless. But it's not the leads. It's whether we have a good strong presentation at the door. Are we smiling? Do we feel confident? Let's say there's a direct mail lead, so you send out a thousand pieces and you'd get maybe 15 back. One agent could take them and do nothing and say the leads are terrible. The next agent cleans up. So, it's not the leads.

DD: *There is a lot of truth in what you're saying. I know one person who is writing quarter million plus a year and then I know another person who is struggling. They are in the same city and the same area. It's like they're working the same people. It's always the bane of recruiters who train agents and want to bring them up as well. Why does this person do it and not the other. But it comes down to the agent.*

NW: It's self awareness. If we can acknowledge a weakness, then we can fix it. There was a publication called Life Insurance Selling or Broker World - I don't know if it exists anymore. There was a person, **John Melginger**. He ran a monthly article and his tagline was, 'How Are You Going To Get Better If You Don't Know You're Sick?' So that analogy carries over to an agent. If there's an agent with a weakness, he has to be aware and if he won't acknowledge that, he will lose confidence at the door or when he asks for that check or puts the data into the system.

If you falter at that point or if you can't see your weakness, then you won't know how are you going to fix it. There are people who complain about the leads a lot of times. They really need to stop and realize that if they have been in this business but are not successful. If they have been plugging away. It has to be them and not the business or industry. Maybe they don't have the sales skills and they need to improve their sales skills or time management skills.

DD: *I was reading a book by Brian Tracy. One thing I learned is to always blame yourself first. Even if you want to blame somebody else, always say 'I am responsible'. The reason he says that is because if you start with yourself first, you will begin to look at yourself and investigate yourself to see what you could do to improve yourself. I think that's a wise standpoint to start with sales.*

NW: Actually, I love delving into all these books like Brian Tracy's, I remember, the first one might have been How To Swim With Sharks Without Getting Eaten Alive. I've read all of them - Tony Robbins, Og Mandino. Reading all these books makes you a better person. I had gotten away from that, almost like I didn't need those books. But I went back to them - which is in this phase of my life - and realized they, along with YouTube, are incredible resources. These things helped reignite a fire within me. I would suggest all agents read those books and stay with it. I did the Dale Carnegie Course and Toastmasters. I did everything that I could because I knew I had a weakness which was lack of the ultimate confidence to succeed. It took a lot of time. In the beginning you could run on enthusiasm and that works.

DD: Yes, that's important too. I want to go back to the point you made earlier about how you set appointments. You don't pre-qualify. So, to play devil's advocate here, why not pre-qualify? Certainly you're running appointments where your Medicare people are on oxygen and you can't help. Why cast a broad net versus get really specific on the phone and only see people who are high odds buyers?

NW: Well, I can walk out the door fast if everything's taken care of and there's nothing that I can do to help you, even if you wanted me to. But I want as many opportunities to sell in a day as possible. I don't have a problem selling. It's a system. I can walk out the door every day and have leads. So the biggest problem agents have is sitting at home or in their office. You need to keep moving, keep grinding.

DD: Do you think that if one has more appointments, even though they're not qualified, there are more opportunities that present themselves since you are constantly in motion and see more people?

NW: Yes. It makes sense. I think that you get more swings of the bat. It also depends on the areas you go. There are times you'll walk into a home and there might be four or five other people with that person or several generations living in the same home. I do tend to stay away from writing the younger people because I don't want to go fully underwritten insurance. I'll do it for myself or for somebody in my family, but I don't want to get into writing a quarter million dollar term policy. However, I do want to catch the neighbor who's there every day having coffee. So there are a lot of opportunities that present themselves if you're active.

DD: *What are the most common objections that you or your appointment setter experience and what do you say to rebuttal?*

NW: Well, I do have my telemarketer send me two recorded phone calls every day and I've made thousands of calls myself over the years. So the usual objections are 'I already have an agent'. We say, 'That's fine. We're going to come by to make sure everything's working for you and that there are no changes in the Medicare rules that have occurred. Having said that, would morning or afternoon be better for you? OR - We're going to have somebody in your area tomorrow and we'd like to have them stop'. So you go back to that morning or afternoon narrative.

It doesn't matter what the objection is. You should restate the objection and go for one more close. 'I already have an agent' is probably the most common objection we run into. Some people say their health prevents them from making the change. Maybe you want to listen to that one.

DD: *As a quick side note here for the listeners - I did a training session on appointment setting for final expense agents the other day and I spent 20 minutes pounding into the brains of the agents that they have to close for the appointment after each rebuttal. Nick here says he closes with 'would morning or afternoon be better'. So, somebody is going to see me, that is going to be in the morning or afternoon. That's why he's got so many appointments set up.*

NW: The 'morning or afternoon' is called the 'fatal alternative' in most of the sales books I've read over the years. Definitely no "yes or no" questions.

DD: *It's psychology. I have an agent who does annuity reviews, and he made that little change you suggested. He got around 10 appointments in three hours. It works really well.*

You mentioned earlier that you do telemarketing leads and I am on record for not liking telemarketing leads whatsoever. How are your telemarketing leads different than what you would buy through vendor? Why do you prefer them more than, say another source, like direct mail maybe being more common?

NW: I do like direct mail and I use it. Certain times of the year it's more telemarketing. I get some FMO help during the Medicare season to do direct mail. Maybe I do a 3000 direct mail piece this month to shake it up. Direct mail are clearly the better leads and I like showing up to the door with that piece in my hand. What I do is I photocopy an eight and half by 11 sheet of paper on my clipboard and I'll show it to them. A clipboard makes me look professional. Then I'll say, 'You sent this in and I'm here to go over the information'. I only door knock the direct mail doors. I never call a direct mail lead. After all, if you call and they reject you, are you not going to go see them? You're still going to go see them. So why not just go see them? Perhaps it makes sense to grab the low hanging fruit on the phone. I just don't bother.

DD: Yes. We all have our stylistic preferences. The wrong way is not doing anything. So do a little bit of everything. Telemarketing is just one.

NW: Yes, definitely. I've worked many direct mail leads over the years. A long time ago when I first started in this business, one of the things that I did was mortgage insurance, which is either decreasing term insurance or a universal life or whole life. We had this one piece that said 'there's a monster in your mortgage'. They showed a picture of a monster with its hands shoving dollar bills in its mouth with Midland National life insurance company, which is a fantastic life insurance company. So we ran that 'monster in the mortgage' piece to death and it got like 3% responses. So, I used to live and die by a direct mail. Telemarketing is just inexpensive for me.

DD: You hire the telemarketer directly, right?

NW: That's correct. I do enjoy the personal relationship of in-house telemarketers. I can manage the telemarketers who work for me and communicate with them. I think that they do a better job for you if they have some interaction with you. I don't recall contracting out telemarketing leads successfully. Then you always wonder what the person said or if you have a real lead.

DD: Yes. A vendor's job is to make a sale, right? Just like our job is to make a sale. But the problem is that there's a disconnect. You don't quite know.

NW: Right. Agents are suspicious of the vendor who's providing the telemarketer leads. Right out of the gate, the radar is up and it's like 'I know I'm going to get ripped off, I'm going to spend thousands of dollars on these leads and they're going to be no good.' That might be a pessimistic viewpoint that people have, but base in reality.

DD: I'm interested to hear how you run your actual sales presentation. How do you do it? Do you go in and are friendly with these people for like 15, 20 minutes? Do you get right to the point of presentation? Are you going to write in for a medicare supplement type of sale or are you more fact-finder approach? How you do it?

NW: My first question is, 'How is your health?' People are fine to talk about their health because it's probably the one thing they think about each day above all else except for their family. They'll tell me about their health and say something about visiting the doctor. I'll ask how much they paid when they visited the doctor. That may tell me a lot right there, especially if it's somebody in the home and whether they have medicare advantage versus a medicare supplement. If they have a medicare supplement they'll say they have paid for the first time they see a doctor each year but after that they don't pay anything. This tells me they have a plan G. If they say they have paid nothing ever, they have plan F. If they say they pay 5 dollars for a Dr visit, I know it's between three plans. Then I ask how much they paid the specialist. I narrow it down to the exact plan they have. I've not asked them anything about insurance yet.

They may start talking about money and you may stumble upon something there. I'm weaving through this maze and, though it's a series of questions, they aren't invasive. It's more conversational. Some people will say they're fine. I'll ask about their medications and you'll find out the opposite is true.

I don't have a track I run on from the standpoint of a sequence of questions. I'm more conversational and friendly about it. I talk to them and, in the first couple minutes, I know what plans they have without them even knowing it. I'll ask them if they are happy with their coverage. I'll figure out if they have an agent. I'll say, 'You obviously have an agent taking care of you.' If they say no, then that's a good thing, for me.

They might also say they do have an agent. I'll ask when was the last time they saw him? They might say they haven't seen him. So somebody could say, well, I have an agent already and you could buy into that, and it might deter you from pushing. I have a rule of thumb. If they do have an agent who visits them every year, I know they're coming back. If they like the agent, I know not to bother selling that person because the agent's going to come back. You will lose the sales because the other agent gets the last word.

Agents are very protective with Medicare. You get into final expense, a lot of agents are hit it and get it as you well know. But, at the same time, I do want to know if they have an agent and if there's a strong relationship. I'll write it and as soon as that agent catches wind of it, they're going to be right back in that house and tell him how bad of a person I am for doing what I've done to them. I lose my commission or advance - it's not worth it.

DD: *So you never replace existing coverage if there's an agent in a home?*

NW: I do. If I go in a particular area where we have debit companies that are still active, I don't care. They have an agent and usually with the debit companies, it's a new agent every year anyhow. So it doesn't matter. Or if they have several other companies, I'll say, 'I'm sure that was a nice person. But what's important is your wallet, wouldn't you agree?' It's unfortunate because that person probably is with a company they don't realize are overcharging customers for their insurance. There are certain companies whose premiums may be 30 percent higher. I'm going to take that business because they're overpaying and I can help. So, you're wading through this in a conversational manner asking questions. Common sense should prevail.

DD: *You figure their knowledge base, the kind of Medicare supplement they have, and generally what kind of life insurance product they have. Obviously if the person comes by every month that increases the premium. You're dealing with something that's probably pretty pricey.*

NW: I have a transition to other products. I start with Medicare, then go to Final Expense. If they have an agent and everything is good. I'll compliment them perhaps along the lines of, "You've made some good decisions and I would not change anything with that Medicare. We would like to help you in any way we can. What other insurances are you paying for every month? Or what other insurance companies are taking money out of your checking account every month'. Nine times out of 10 it's life insurance. I put my head down, get my pen in my hand and ask who that insurance is with?

Then the conversation is broached. If I pitch the Medicare and I lose, then I am a loser in the eyes of the client. It's important that I don't try and sell one product unsuccessfully before moving onto another. I want to make the transition to Final Expense after giving them a compliment on there medicare purchase decision. I'll mention that some people pay for accident policies or cancer policies and so on. They might say only life insurance. Again, I've got pen to paper and I'm ready to move down that path.

DD: *So it's not canned.*

NW: Right. It's not canned. I find if I have a buyer and if I see that there's an opportunity, I wait for them to tell me how to solve it. I'm not going to push. I'm going to sit back and wait until something is brought up that enables me to go there.

For example. If I get my prospect to that point when they say that they have an agent and then later they have some complains about him. That's something I can proceed with..

DD: Yes, no doubt. I mean, you find you've got a company that has a 50 percent higher price for life insurance. Certainly there's your angle. So your job is to go in and find the angle between one of the options that you have. You make a presentation, try to sell it if you can. How long does your average sales call last? If you make the sale and then if you don't make the sale, how long is it until you pack up and you're out the door?

NW: I usually pack up real fast - 10 to 15 minutes. I don't hang out in a house. I ask a few questions and I know what they have, so what's the point of hanging around? Sometimes it's five minutes. I don't want to be rude though. I think it's rude to abruptly get up and leave. I'll tell them along the lines of 'well I can't make any money here' - making a joke and I want to get down the road. They don't mind that. They'll laugh and they'll agree. But if I can sell, I'm going to stay there as long as I have to.

If I can make a sale there, then that's the most valuable home on that day so I stay there until I get a buying signal. Now, they are comfortable that they got their person. Then you can proceed and wrap things up and move on.

There is no technical presentation at that point. The technical presentation is going to get you the sale but it's going to get you the cancellation. Most of my business, even the final expense business I write, will stick. Of course you always get surprised at that final expense. I mean, potentially you never know where it's going to come from.

DD: So you've been in this business for 30 years now. You've seen all sorts of agents come and go. If we look at the agent who is new to this business, do you think that their focus should be on representing one product or possibly cross selling from the start? If they shouldn't cross sell, when do you think they should start?

NW: I believe that you should learn several products. Certainly you've got to know final expense upfront because that's how you're going to feed the family. New agents have to know how to sell final expense insurance and they need to get to that medicare advantage season and kill it. I believe the easier lead is the Medicare and the easy spinoff is the final expense. So if you're very adept at spinning off final expense, you'll be good. I would not worry about getting into anything else as a new agent. Perhaps the hospital Indemnity insurance.

You see companies that advertise single premium life and annuities. I would not worry about that if I'm a new agent at all. I would turn it over to somebody else. You can go down that rabbit hole but it's a time drain. You have got to be proficient at doing the the medicare to Final Expense transition. That is a transition that works, that's the only one I use.

Final expense insurance is not that complicated, neither is Medicare, once you got a good grasp of them. Maybe when you get into Medicare advantage, the laws and rules, the co-pays, co-insurance and deductibles, can be complicated. If you're a professional, you should learn your profession. You should pound in the books at night. There should be no reason that you don't know exactly how final expense works and how to compare final expense products and how to sell final expense expense products.

DD: How do you close your sales presentation? What do you ask? How do you present the solution you're going to sell them via Medicare or final expense? How do you deal with the objection?

NW: Generally, I tell people what to do so I don't ask them. I'll tell you a story. This was when I was a rookie agent. One of the things I did was to sell individual health insurance to small business owners. I was selling to this person who owned a tire brokerage, he ran out of his house. He sold tires all over the world from his home.

I went in giving details about $200 deductible and $1,000 deductible and start telling them all about different options he had, to the point of overkill. And he asks, 'Who taught you how to sell? I want you to pack up your bags and go back and tell your manager to teach you how to sell. You shouldn't ask me what I want to do. Don't give me all these options. Tell me what's best for me. Tell me what to do. If I knew what to do, I wouldn't need you.'

It's not like I immediately changed. But that person taught me a lesson and now I don't ask anybody what to do. I say, 'Here's the problem, here's how we're going to fix it. What I need to do to get started is this. First we need to make sure that you qualify. I'm going to go through these medical questions to make sure you're accepted and then we're going to call your existing company. We're going to stop the bank draft you have to that other company. We won't cancel the policy, just stop the bank draft until we are 100% certain the new plan is approved and everything is acceptable to you."

If they're comfortable, I'll say, 'Let's call the underwriting department. They're going to do a review and they're going to tell us whether you're approved or not

I like to call it 'maintaining an authoritative presence."

DD: So what happens if they object? Let's say they object even if you have a medicare deal that can save them money. How do you deal with it?

NW: A lot of times it goes back to change. I sit with the seniors and go over the same scenario as I have with you now. They won't change it. Do you know why? It's because they're afraid to change. So I'll tell them, 'You're successful person. You've got a nice home here. You've obviously made some good decisions. At what point is it that you decided to stop making good decisions?'

When seniors turn age 65 or they get into Medicare, for some reason they stopped making those good decisions and there's no reason not to save money. It's not that they don't like what you've said or they don't like you. They probably liked what you said and it probably makes sense. But they are knuckled down because they don't want to change. But I want to let them know that it's OK to change.

You probably know if you do a good presentation, you don't usually get a lot of kickbacks. Almost every sale I make is a one call close. Because I'm taking my time if I see that there's a sale to be made. I'm going to camp out and I'm going to wait until it all make sense and then I'm going to close it. Another agent could probably close faster, but not better.

DD: What do you think are the common threads between the successful agents that stay in this business? You've seen agents come and go. Why do people fail? What are your thoughts on that?

NW: Even if you're at your desk, you have to mentally pack that cooler and go to work like anybody else. Agents get into bad habits because they don't work hard enough. I believe that you should get as many leads as you can and get out there and start selling. So if you're selling final expense, get the cheapest leads you can get and grind it. You can buy old direct mail and show up at the door, pull out that card and say, 'Hey, you sent this in a while back. I don't know if anybody's taken care of you. I wanted to stop by and see if I could help you out.'

Agents usually start out fine, for the first six months. Once we get going, we get overwhelmed. We have the business management side of it, time management, lead management, piles of paper on our desk that aren't moving properly.

If you're not practicing your craft and being the best that you can be, you will struggle and then switch to another lead source because you didn't improve your skill set enough to continue down the road. Gradually and eventually, you'll be out of the business. You'll get by in the beginning on enthusiasm, but then the enthusiasm starts to wane.

When I started, we would literally call out of the the white pages. I remember making sales out of the white pages. I would call new neighborhoods or a new subdivision and say, "This is Nick Williams, I help people with mortgage insurance in your community. Since your a new homeowner in that I want to do is stop by and help you out with your insurance. We have a program that will pay for the home if either you or your spouse passes away and if you live, it'll pay off your home early with the cash value." I've made that call 10,000 times.

DD: Please tell us how to contact you and where can we find more about you?

NW: I have the Medicare Millionaire Facebook page and Medicare Millionaire YouTube channel. Our website is www.medicaremillionaire.com.

Is A Career Selling Insurance A Racket?

Ryan Madison interviews David Duford

RM: Before I began selling final expense insurance, I was interested in learning more about the industry. I stumbled across a YouTube channel that gave me several kinds of tips and training on selling final expense insurance. Since then, I've used that training to help me increase my production. I appreciate this gentleman's dedication to helping agents like me who have brought no monetary gain. I don't have any contracts through him and I don't pay him for training. All I've done is watch free content on YouTube and read his blogs. They are absolutely top notch. Our guest today has over 3,000 subscribers on YouTube, over 500 training videos, many of which have over 10,000 views. He is the author of the book, The Official Guide To Selling Final Expense Insurance. Please welcome David Duford. ***Dave, tell us about yourself.***

DD: I have been in the insurance business since 2011 and I started out of complete desperation. I had a business prior to this which was affected by the Great Recession. I stumbled across the final expense business and jumped in. I certainly had my ups my downs. Now I recruit agents nationally and train them in my Mentorship Program.

RM: I can definitely attest to that because you do help a lot of people. Tell us a little bit of your background. Where did you grow up, where do you live, what made you get into the industry, and how long have you been in the industry?

DD: I grew up in a town called Chattanooga, Tennessee about two hours north of Atlanta. My parents are from Michigan. I graduated from Boston University. I was interested in the fitness business and I had a personal training gym. I was in my early twenties and things were going great. Then, unfortunately, the bottom fell out of the market. Most of my clients were from upper and middle upper income groups and they realized that their retirements were being dramatically affected.

I had in mind to become a business owner and enjoy the freedom that comes along with running a business. I couldn't get a job. Then I came across insurance. I stumbled across the final expense business and liked how it was a high first year commission product. I didn't need to learn any advanced information like with Medicare or annuities. It was primarily a numbers related business. I decided to jump in part time to see if it was right for me. Once I got some traction, I went all in.

RM: Are you mostly training the agents?

DD: I transitioned to support and mentor my agency for the hundreds who work with me across the country. As of 2018, I do sell on the field although not full time. It averages to about a day a week and most of that is done when I have agents come with me to be trained in the field. They come with leads and I coach them to improve their sales skills. In conjunction with that, there are some deals or referrals I might pick up on those days.

RM: How many agents would you say you have trained or help train? You have a pretty big audience on YouTube.

DD: I don't know the exact number but around five hundred. Not all of them are going to do business, some of them will contract and not pull the first trigger. It's normal. There is a core group that does some business on a constant basis. At some point or another in the last five years of training, I've worked with at least 500 to 600 agents who have come through the doors that has done some kind of business or at least attempted to.

RM: That's great. Where can our listeners find you on social media?

DD: The best place is YouTube because that's where I focus all my efforts. You can YouTube search "Dave Duford" or "Final Expense Agent Mentor" and you'll find me.

RM: Why do you do it and how long have you been doing that?

DD: When I started recruiting early on, it was strictly for final expense. And most of the recruiting other organizations were doing was focused on multi-level marketing. It was not based on skill development and agent development. I looked at it with a different angle. Not everybody wants to recruit a down line. Others want to write with their own pen and to create a business that has both an upside potential and gives them the freedom they desire. But they want the training and the support that comes along with it too.

That is where I stuck my flag. It naturally evolved into a YouTube channel. There were not many resources in the market then. So it dawned on me that this was a good way to position my agency and create connections with people. I can show people on YouTube - like Frank Kern talks about "results in advance" - how to handle objections or how to effectively sell final expense.

At this point in 2018, it has evolved into more than final expense. I speak a lot about insurance sales training for any insurance professional who needs help with building rapport or presenting effectively. The product doesn't matter. I do interviews like this one now. It's evolving into a wider breadth of products and knowledge. The training helps all insurance agents with the goal of improving knowledge that agents can put into force and good use.

RM: Exactly. We share a common vision as far as acquiring and improving knowledge is concerned. I agree with your assessment that the level of training available is abysmal. Everything seems to be so hushed, which is

the reason we created this show. We want to be able to spread some knowledge which everybody needs to be successful.

I want to talk about a couple of your shows, which is the topic of today's show. Your most popular videos are 'Why Life Insurance Careers Are A Racket', 'Learn The Truth About Selling Final Insurance'. What is your vision for Final Expense Agent Mentor? Are your videos facing consumers or agents. Are they for new agents who are coming into the industry or for agents who are already in the industry and feel like they are part of a racket? Can you explain?

DD: I'm sure your audience is wondering why you are talking to a person who thinks that selling insurance is a racket even though he sells insurance.

The main emphasis of that video is directed towards this unfortunate bias and interaction that the insurance agencies tilt toward the multilevel marketing system. It's not a problem with the product of insurance, but with the distribution style. It's all based on personal sales or referrals of your friends and family, and then trying to recruit some of those people to duplicate the process. You develop a long down line and build a passive income.

But, the problem in insurance we see is that these companies cannot get through an introductory meeting at the agency without being pitched on recruiting. You realize you don't even know which insurance companies you are representing or what your clients are going to say. What happens is that the quality of the training and the knowledge base lowers continuously over time to the point where consumers don't get the kind of service or help that they should get. This gives us a bad name. It establishes a perspective that somebody selling insurance is not a professional like a doctor or an accountant who has knowledge and skills that can be measurably taught and positively affect somebody's life.

It is great for the people who are at the top of the pyramid, but it's the worst option for the people who are in the trenches and want a system that will help them succeed.

RM: I know. What do you suggest new agents do when they are thinking about getting a career in insurance? What steps should they take to make sure that they are not put into an indoctrination of some sort of recruiting cult? I agree with you that the training drops off when somebody with four months or a year of experience is going to teach them the right way to do it. They need to learn from somebody with decades of experience. Would you agree with that?

DD: The hiring practices in the insurance business are entirely different from corporate America in the sense that if you have a pulse, 9 out of 10 agencies will hire you. Why do they do that? Because their strategy, in most cases, is to do what's called a Project 100 or 200. Create a list of friends, family members, business associates. The concept is to recruit and to develop business from them. That works for a short time. But how would you find business and prospect when you exhaust that list?

So acknowledge that you should have the discernment when you're looking for an agency instead of falling for the first person in a suit who tells you that you're the best thing since sliced bread. He is telling you what you want to hear and then tries to entice you into being a member of their organization. But you have to interview him. That's the strategy you have to employ. They meet the profile of what you need to be successful.

As a new agent you have to find somebody who knows their business inside out. You should work with somebody who has field experience. People who recruit have a different set of experiences that the people who sell. I prefer to work with people who experientially understand the selling process.

RM: They will help agents better versus the marketer who is going to capture agencies. I always ask my mentor how he is going to help me get in front of people. He said 'go out there and learn the system. Interview, ask everybody and see what you think is going to be the best fit for you'. He warned me about the project 100 and the project 250. He said they continued to do it and that has become the status quo. Imagine you have a giant plate of spaghetti in front of you. Grab a big handful of that spaghetti and throw it against the wall and see who sticks. You have a bunch of

spaghetti strings at first. But quite quickly they all fall down on the ground with maybe one or two left. Well, all those agents whom they brought in and asked to work on project 100. You write that business underneath somebody else's name because you're in training. Then you fall out of the business 6 months later, but they have all your family and friends on their insurance plans. So they win for those people who do stay in the business, even if you fall out of the business. It doesn't seem to be the best for agents to do like that.

So what's your vision for Final Expense Agent Mentor and where do you see it in five years?

DD: I will continue to expand my agency and work with selected agents who want to dedicate themselves to selling not only final expense but also other product lines. One of the goals I have for next year or two is to start differentiating our offerings. My agency is moving from niche to a broader base approach and we're going to keep working that angle. We're going to be rolling out more training that relates to health insurance agents, helps them master the selling and marketing process to be successful in this business.

RM: We have one big question that we ask our guests. There are so many different facets of the insurance industry. Why did you choose to specialize in final expense? What inspired you to start with final expense?

DD: My mindset was that I didn't want to spend months preparing either for certifications or credentials. I wanted to avoid the study process in an advanced product. When I saw Medicare, for example, I thought there was a lot I have to know about Medicare which scared me off since I was new into the insurance business. I wanted a product that had a mass market, applied to a lot of potential prospects, and was simple to sell. That's where I found final expense to be a good start as a new agent. I had all the important things required to show up and work hard. The Baby Boomer market is huge, 10,000 a day for the next 20 to 30 years. There is going to be a never ending supply of people who are thinking about dying that may want a plan.

RM: I personally think that the baby boomer generation is an underserved market. Many of them are getting pitched guaranteed issue and so on from the mail. A lot of times, they pay twice as much as they should. So the final expense agents we work with have some sort of lead program. There is no reason for our seniors, who don't have a lot and have medical issues, to be paying twice as much as they should be on their insurance. I think the shortage of agents is the reason for that. Would you agree that there's a shortage of agents for what the needs are for the consumer base?

DD: Yes. On an average, an insurance agent is 59 or 60 years old. I'm 33. That's great. The need for life insurance is increasing, and the average insurance agent is facing retirement within the next 5 to 10 years. Most people agree that they need life insurance and admit they don't have enough. That puts a great opportunity in the hands of the hardworking agent who will meet people.

RM: Would you suggest new agents to try and get into the final expense realm because it's easier than others?

DD: I think that final expenses is one of those products to be considered because, anytime you make a career change, everything is new. I don't care if you're a great salesperson from the home improvement business or you're coming from business to business sales. Insurance is a different product. You need a product that is easy to run with and is more activity driven than a product that is based on a unique market. Secondly, I suggest mortgage protection. That is also a great product to start. It's a duplicatable product that has a large market. If you like working with older people, final expense is a good option.

RM: So final expenses is simple, straightforward, and basic because there are not a lot of moving parts. Whereas you go into something like an annuity which is complicated. So you say that mortgage protection is as simple as final expense or is that a little bit more advanced?

DD: I think mortgage protection, like final expense, is selling a particular type of need. It's easy to understand for most people. The idea is to to say, for instance, that the prospect has got $150,000 mortgage but what if he dies? How will that affect your surviving spouse or the income? Mortgage protection has added benefits. When people file for mortgage loans, they know that they are in debt and the situation after their passing certainly crosses their mind. So simple products like that are a great way to get started.

I think it's also important to add, focus only on one product. Don't get down in the weeds trying to sell everything to everybody. The best agents whom I know go on conventions, focus on one product. There are agents who do a little bit of everything and do it well, but a lot of the best producers are specialists. At the beginning, give yourself a year to become a master before you start thinking of annuities or similar complicated insurances because you will get distracted. Diffusion is the enemy of productivity.

RM: I think what also happens is if you're not confident, you won't be able to write much. If you're confused on how annuity works and you try to write one, you can stumble if somebody wants to shift over 50 to 100,000. All of a sudden your credibility with them plummets.

DD: Undoubtedly. There are compliance issues with some of these products and you shouldn't ruin somebody's retirement, especially if you don't have a base point yet. Of course, you have to eventually launch something and then take a step out and give it a shot. You're not going to know everything until you do it, especially if you're new. A simple product like life insurance, mortgage protection, term insurance, voluntary payroll deduct or final expense are easily understood products that a lot of people need.

RM: Let's talk about the Inner Circle program. Can you fill us in?

DD: Absolutely. A significant part of my business focuses on training agents who want to work within my agency. I recognized that there were a lot of people who enjoyed my content on Youtube and in my email newsletter. They were happy enough with the current setup of their organization, but they realized the importance of additional training. That was the seed of the Inner Circle concept. I decided to create a program to help agents by streaming live coaching sessions where agents could listen to me train on a subject. Many times I review live sales calls from real life agents, live prospecting calls by the agents.

The Inner Circle also facilitates a community amongst agents who are passionate about education so they can advance in their careers. That is the Inner Circle concept. Agents have one-on-one consultation with me every month to talk about whatever burning questions they have about what they are experiencing. There are live coaching calls I take multiple times a month to reinforce their training methods. There's a community on Facebook for private members only encouraging each other by sharing and answering questions. There is also a back end training that has several training modules on all the products we've mentioned earlier if they want to investigate different products.

RM: You made a valuable point which hits home with our topic perfectly. Is a career in insurance a racket? What I see personally is that everyone wants to keep their training to themselves. It sounds like you're trying to break that trend by making training available to people even when you're not going to try to recruit them or get them to switch their contracts over to you. You're there for everybody regardless of the company they are with. Is that what I'm hearing?

DD: Yes. The common mindset is, 'Why would I give out information to my potential competition?' I don't think that we have as much competition as we think. I have been final expense for 7 years and the worst competition that would affect you daily is yourself. If you want to beat your worst competition, then you need better education. You need to have more access to resources and materials to do a better job. The reality is there is endless amount of prospects and you will never get to all of them.

RM: Let's dive into your book for a few minutes. What spurred you to write a book? If you talked to anybody who has written a book before, they usually say that writing a book is dreadful. It's amazing to be an author of a book and selling it, but the actual writing process is daunting. What made you decide to write a book?

DD: Yes, writing a book is daunting. It is a time commitment. It took me two years to get to the end of it, not because there were a lot of details but because I put it on my shelf for a year and a half since it took a lot of my time. The reason I have a book is because people learn using different resources. Some people are comfortable with YouTube videos, some learn a lot from podcasts. I have what's called the Picard Syndrome. I used to watch Star Trek: The Next Generation where Captain Picard couldn't stand reading e-books. He had to feel the book cover. That is what spurred me on.

RM: I cannot wait to read your book. You had mentioned before to focus on one thing. There is a book by Gary Keller called 'The One Thing' in which he goes deep into the reasons to focus on one thing. How often do you read?

DD: I have set a goal of reading 50 to 60 books in 2018. I'm probably at about 30 books. I am an avid reader. I admit though that like anything in life, you have to discipline yourself. I have to schedule reading first thing in the morning or last thing at night. I read only 30 minutes a day, but if you commit yourself to that, you become a good reader which makes you become a good leader. The financial opportunities usually come from that.

RM: I'm an advocate for self education and my advice to everybody is that when you're in your car, listen to Dave on Youtube. I am sure listening to that might turn your car into a mobile university. A lot of times when you're doing final expense, you want to maximize your time. Are you doing it as you could as time comes up?

DD: I'm a sincere advocate for listening to Brian Tracy. Brian Tracy is a management guru. My favorite material by Brian is time management. I like how he teaches to schedule your work day. I determined that in the beginning of the year I was going to commit to a long term reading schedule. I might read an hour a week, but I could get triple or quadruple the amount of time if I would set aside time.

I do it first thing in the morning before the day starts. I do it at the end of the day after the kids are in bed. Either way, if you want to do anything in life and you want to make it a priority, you have to put it down in writing and you have to make it your goal to eliminate everything in your schedule so that you feel productive.

RM: It's something that has to develop as a habit. I'm fortunate that I was given very good advice to begin reading and self-educating when I started my bachelor's in business. During my four years studying business at college, I was also reading books and it made the work easier because I was well versed on the different ins and outs. If it's worth doing once a week, it's worth doing every day. If you do it every day, you'll build the habit and you'll be surprised when you look back over the last three years because you may have read 150 books. How many books do you think you've read?

DD: Over the years, I've read over 100 books. I'm naturally lazy, but have a grasp on discipline. One of the things about being an entrepreneur is you're on your own! Nobody's going to motivate you to go work. I have to be my own boss. Get serious about setting daily goals.

RM: Yes. Let's talk about some final remarks here. What do you think is the biggest challenge in the industry right now for the new agents?

DD: To survive. I think that's the key thing. I think it was Al Granum, one of these old school legends of selling insurance, who said that the goal is to survive this business because if you can survive selling insurance, things start to turn the corner. I talked about my failure within the first year. I failed out of the business because of silly mistakes I did. But I had a chance to get back in. I realize that my life would have been an absolute disaster if I had to work for corporation that cared less about me and wanted me to push a product that I didn't believe in.

It's a clear goal as to what you want to accomplish in your career and it's about sticking to the plan. Part of what's important about that plan is having people to present to. I don't care what people think or say. This is a numbers game. You've have to see the people and you have to do it every week and stay consistent to it.

RM: Would you agree that it comes down to training?

DD: I'm not saying that the only solution is that it's a numbers game, but I think there's a balance to training and as well as activity. If Mr. Charismatic is doing only two or three final expense presentations a week, but my salesperson, who is moderately skilled, is doing 15, he's going to do much better.

RM: You mentioned 15 appointments a week. Is that what your average agents are doing?

DD: That depends on the part time to full time. I think that 15 is the magic number. There are people in our industry and final expense who talk about 15 appointments a week thing - the magic number. There's a book called 'It Can Only Get Better'. The author - Tony Gordon - learned the magic 15 number early on in his career.

The concept is simple. See 15 people a week. If you see 15 people a week, things tend to happen. Of course, nobody's going to tell you it's going to be some sort of algorithmic predictable equation. But generally speaking, if you could do 15 appointments a week, you're going to make sales and get new opportunities.

RM: Well, we are coming to the end of our show here. How can our listeners learn more details about final expense agent mentor?

DD: I think the best way to get to know me better is to go to my YouTube channel. Type in my name, Dave Duford, or Final Expense Agent Mentor. And go ahead and subscribe! YouTube allows me the greatest opportunity for you to get to know me and what I preach.

About Dave Duford

Dave Duford is self-described "Renaissance Man" in the insurance business, licensed as a life insurance agent since 2011. Dave sells primarily final expense face-to-face and over-the-phone, recruits and mentors new and experienced agents nationally, and is the author of the best-selling final expense book, "The Official Guide To Selling Final Expense."

Dave also operates a highly-successful YouTube channel, where he teaches sales and prospecting training to insurance agents. YouTube Search "Dave Duford" for more information.

In addition, Dave operates "Insurance Agent Inner Circle," a monthly membership program designed to help new and experienced agents with mentoring, coaching, live video training, and insurance niche training in final expense, mortgage protection, Medicare Supplements, and annuity sales training. See the following page for more information.

Dave lives in Chattanooga, Tennessee, with his wife, Laura, and his four kids, and for fun, and enjoys getting tapped out in Brazilian Jiu-Jitsu.

You can learn more about Dave Duford at www.FEAgentMentor.com.

www.MortgageProtectionAgentMentor.com

Books By David Duford, Available On Amazon & As E-Books At The Websites Above

The Official Guide To Selling Final Expense Insurance
The Official Guide To Buying Final Expense Life Insurance

Special Free Gift From Dave Duford...

The Most Incredible FREE Gift Ever

INSURANCE AGENT INNER CIRCLE

Take advantage of this offer at https://goo.gl/Tsvjpk

Here's what you'll get:

'Elite' Insurance Agent Inner Circle Membership (1 Month Value = $79.00)

IAIC Benefits Include:

- Weekly **"Ask Dave Anything"** Live, On-Camera Insurance Sales Training Calls
- **Monthly 1-on-1 Coaching Calls** With Dave To Answer Any & All Insurance Sales, Marketing, & Prospecting Questions You Have
- **Ride-Along Training Opportunities** To Help You Sell More Insurance
- **Access To 5 Insurance Sales & Marketing Systems** (Final Expense, Medicare Supplements, Mortgage Protection, Annuity Sales, Critical Illness)
- **Facebook Insurance Lead Generation For Newbies Video Course**
- **Dave's Official Guide To Developing Insurance Websites** That Send You Hot Leads.
- **Insurance Carrier Reviews** For Over 50 Insurance Products

Take advantage of this offer at https://goo.gl/Tsvjpk

There is a one-time membership activation fee of $9.99 to get you started on the FREE month's access to the Insurance Agent Inner Circle Program. Once your activation fee is processed at the website above, you will automatically continue at the lowest Inner Circle price of $69.00 per month. Should you decide to cancel your membership, you can do so at any time by emailing support@feagentmentor.com. Remember, you will NOT be charged the low monthly membership fee until the end of the first month of your Inner Circle Membership, which means you'll receive 30 days to read and profit from all the powerful techniques and strategies you get from being an Inner Circle Member. And of course, it's impossible for you to lose, because if you don't absolutely LOVE everything you get, you can simply cancel your membership at any time during the first month of membership and never get billed a single penny.

Made in the USA
Lexington, KY
19 August 2018